ARE YOU AN INCLUSIVE
DESIGNER?

Julie Fleck has been advising on the creation of an accessible and inclusive environment for over 30 years. As the Principal Access and Inclusive Design Adviser at the Greater London Authority she was responsible for the inclusive design and accessible housing policies in the London Plan, and following the London 2012 Olympic and Paralympic Games was seconded to the Office for Disability Issues as the Project Lead for the Government's Paralympic Legacy BEPE Project (the Built Environment Professional Education Project). She is a Design Council Built Environment Expert, a member of British Standards B/559 Committee, and in 2004 was awarded the OBE for services to disabled people.

ARE YOU AN INCLUSIVE
DESIGNER?

Julie Fleck

RIBA ✛ Publishing

Contents

Dedication   8
Acknowledgements   8
Preface   12

Introduction

**A celebration of inclusion or a warning against   13
complacency?**

Chapter 1

How much have we achieved in 50 years?   21
Half a century of technical standards   23
Design for special needs   25
The first legislation to address access to buildings   28
The social model of disability   30
The Access Committee for England   32
The first planning policies   33
Design and Access Statements   38
The London Plan   40
The first building regulation   46
The principles of inclusive design   49
Civil rights legislation   53
We still have a long way to go to achieve inclusion   56

Chapter 2

Designing an accessible City   61
The inaccessible City   63
Access Adaptations Programme   64
    Improved access to the Great Hall, Guildhall   67
    Improving access to green spaces   75

City of London Access Group   77
    Dropped kerbs and tactile paving   78
Guidelines for an accessible built environment   81
Have we now achieved 'an accessible City'?   82
    Getting to and around London   85
    Despite improvements, barriers to inclusion persist in the City   86
Creating an inclusive environment is a continuous process   90

Chapter 3

The most accessible Olympic and Paralympic Games   **93**
Going above and beyond the regulations   94
The integration of access and inclusion   97
Stratford City Consultative Access Group   98
An inclusive planning process   102
Compliance procedure   104
Disabled people played a key role   105
Welcoming disabled visitors to London   108
An inclusive development process from the outset   112

Chapter 4

The good, the bad and the inaccessible   **119**
The Sill National Landscape Discovery Centre, Northumberland   121
Portway Lifestyle Centre, Sandwell, West Midlands   128
Frank Barnes School for Deaf Children, King's Cross, London   132
Royal Liverpool Philharmonic   140
Storyhouse, Chester   146
HOME, Manchester   156
St Paul's Cathedral, City of London   161
National Army Museum, Chelsea, London   169
Temple of Mithras, City of London   175
The Bank of England Museum, City of London   177
Thames Riverside Walk at Blackfriars Bridge, City of London   179
Up at the O2, Greenwich, London   184
5 Pancras Square, King's Cross, London   187

Library of Birmingham 189
Clink Street, Bankside, London 190
Tower Bridge, London 192
Beach Huts, Boscombe, Bournemouth 193

The devil is in the detail: 196
Tapering steps 196
Foreshortened handrails 198
Open step risers 200
Lack of contrast on step risers and treads 200
Narrow, uneven and cluttered paths 203
Seats without arms and back rests 205
Illegible wayfinding 206
Heavy doors and confusing entrances 208
Highly patterned and shiny surfaces 209

Chapter 5

Towards better legislation, policy and regulations 211

Improvements to legislation, policy and regulations can 213
    accelerate change
    Inclusive design is a critical element of planning policy 214
    Improving the building regulations 217
    Inclusive Design Strategies built into project briefs and 220
      procurement processes
    Opportunities through licensing legislation 224
    Inclusive design is sustainable design 227
Existing, historic and listed buildings can be made accessible 231
The need for more accessible and adaptable housing 234
The drive towards healthy streets 238
A better way to challenge disability discrimination 243
Towards better implementation 245

Chapter 6

Towards an inclusive future   **248**
Changing our behaviour   250
Nothing about us without us   255
    Local and strategic access groups   255
    Collective and co-production   257
Is ignorance the enemy of inclusion?   258
    The Built Environment Professional Education Project (BEPE) 259
    New initiatives to improve skills and knowledge 264
Encouraging clients to embrace an inclusive design approach   269
    Missing out on £249 billion   269
The Dairy, Cottage in the Dales   272
    The impact of lottery funding   276
    Missing out on talent   278
    Inclusion champions   279
Looking forward to an inclusive future   281
Are you an inclusive designer?   283

Conclusion   289

Appendices

Appendix 1   **294**
Stratford City Consultative Access Group:
    Protocol for Accessible Presentations
Appendix 2   **299**
Stratford City Consultative Access Group:
Protocol for Written Material
Appendix 3   **300**
Stratford City Consultative Access Group:
    Lessons learnt and transferability to other projects

Abbreviations   301
Bibliography   304
Further information   307
Notes and References   309
Index   325
Image credits   334

Dedication

To Caroline Gooding and Andrew Walker
They dedicated their lives to challenging disability discrimination and promoting equality. Their wonderful friendship and invaluable support gave me the courage and enthusiasm to spend my career working to achieve a more inclusive environment. I miss them both.

Acknowledgments

It is hard to know where to begin as there are so many people I want to thank, not just for giving me the inspiration to write this book, but also for helping and encouraging me in my career as an access officer and inclusive design advisor – they are the reason I could write this book at all.

I should start with Andrew Walker, who I first met at a British Standards Institution (BSI) meeting in 1989 and who, through his dogged determination, demonstrated how to defy what was then expected of a 'disabled' person. I have very fond memories of the many conversations I had with him over a glass of red wine watching him cook a delicious stew in his basement kitchen, in his very inaccessible Georgian house converted into one exclusively designed to meet his own particular needs as a wheelchair user and his aesthetic demands as a conservation architect. In 1993 he ran the first postgraduate course on what was then termed Environmental Access at the Architectural Association and he had a major influence on the development of inclusive design principles and processes in the UK.

I also want to thank all the friends and colleagues who worked tirelessly during the 1990s, the decade when, I believe, the most progress was made, particularly those who went on to work for and make the Disability Rights Commission a driving force for change. I first met Caroline Gooding when she worked at RADAR (the Royal Association of Disability and Rehabilitation) and I was a member of the Access Committee for England (ACE). Her reputation for developing the legal framework for the Disability Discrimination Act is well known, but she was also very supportive of those of us determined to put built environment access firmly on the government agenda and I truly valued her friendship. Peter Lainson, Sabrina Aaronovitch, Clare Goodridge and Alun Francis made my time as a member of ACE really enjoyable. They all taught me a lot and are still friends today.

'Nothing about us without us' has always been central to my approach at work and I could not have achieved nearly as much without the dedication, hard work and friendship of all the local access groups I have worked with. These are too numerous to name individually, but Peter Barker, director of the Joint Mobility Unit at the Royal Institute of Blind People (from 1992 to 2001), was particularly helpful when I first started working for the Corporation of London. I learnt a lot from the members of the City of London Access Group and when I moved to the Greater London Authority (GLA) I enjoyed being frequently challenged by members of the London Access Forum. A big thank you goes to Peter Lainson, who chaired both the Access Committee for England and later the London

Access Forum. Without his leadership and his challenging and pertinent contributions, neither organisation would have had the influence they had.

The highlight of my career was, of course, working on the planning process for the London 2012 Olympic and Paralympic Games, so a huge thank you is due to all the members of the Olympic Delivery Authority's Built Environment Access Panel (ODA BEAP) and before that the Stratford City Consultative Access Group (SCCAG), along with my professional colleagues at the ODA and GLA – Margaret Hickish, Mark Dyer and David Morris. They all helped to deliver the 'most accessible Olympic and Paralympic Games in history'[1] and encouraged me to further develop the inclusive design planning policies in the London Plan.

I would like to thank my colleagues on the British Standards Institution (BSI) B/559 Committee, particularly David Petherick and Geoff Cook, and at the Access Association – Rachel Smalley, Pippa Jackson and Neil Smith. A special thank you is also due to members of the Built Environment Professional Education Project Board (BEPE), particularly Paul Morrell, whose encouragement helped the project progress way beyond my early expectations.

A huge thank you also goes to all the people who have shared their plans, photographs and other images that have helped bring this book alive (see Image Credits, p 334).

But the most important person to thank is my partner Liz, whose constant love, support and quiet patience behind the scenes sent me off to work every morning with the courage to keep on keeping on. She has had to put up with my anger, frustration and obsession when it seemed that the world was not listening to our demands for a more accessible environment and when I was seeing the impact that physical and attitudinal barriers were having on my friends and colleagues. On many holidays she had no choice but to wait for me to take yet another photograph of an accessible toilet, ramp, handrail or lift. She waited patiently for my company while I hid myself away at the computer trying to put all my thoughts down in this book, and kept me going with all her delicious meals. Thank you, Liz.

I feel incredibly lucky that I have known so many generous and committed people and have been able to spend my working life in their company, working together to try to make a difference to people's lives. As David Morris (the Mayor of London's disability advisor from 2003 to 2009) frequently said, it's hard work trying to change the world, but we must keep on trying.

Preface

This book is not an academic study or the result of years of research, nor is it a technical manual. It is my reflections on how the UK has been addressing the need to make our buildings, places and spaces more accessible to disabled people and what more we can all do to create an inclusive environment.

I have drawn on my personal experience of working for three London local authorities – Wandsworth Borough Council, the Corporation of London (now the City of London Corporation) and the Greater London Authority – followed by a secondment to the civil service, along with my involvement in various national committees promoting better access for disabled people.

Writing this book has reinforced my view about how much more there is to do, not just in terms of improving legislation and technical standards and increasing our own skills and knowledge, but in our understanding of why we still do not build and maintain homes, places of work and entertainment, and parks and open spaces that address and effectively incorporate the access needs of disabled and older people. Understanding the barriers to inclusion may help to change our attitude and our behaviour so that inclusive access becomes standard practice, an integrated and normal part of any planning, design, construction and management process.

Despite the immense improvements I have witnessed in my career as an access and inclusive design advisor, there is still a long way to go before we achieve an inclusive environment where we can all be free to realise our potential.

Introduction

A celebration of inclusion or a warning against complacency?

This book is a celebration – the last 30 years have seen significant improvements to the accessibility of our towns and cities. Disabled people are now far more visible on our streets, in our schools, working in shops and offices and travelling independently on public transport – it is so much easier to get around today than it was 30 or 40 years ago. However, this book is also a warning. A warning against being complacent, as complacency leads to compromise and compromise can lead to exclusion.

Although inclusive design is increasingly being addressed at all stages of the design process in new developments – from inception through to completion and occupation – sadly this approach is still not the norm. Many in the construction industry still think that inclusive design adds to the cost of a development and, as keeping costs to a minimum is a key driver of many schemes, access and inclusion are often not considered until it is too late to maximise the economic benefit of early consideration, when costs can be easily absorbed.

Accessible and inclusive design is also still frequently considered purely as a regulatory requirement, with meeting minimum standards the sole consideration, resulting in a race to the bottom. This attitude leads to a tick-box approach at the end of the design process and can result in costly alterations to plans during the planning process or building control stage, with expensive but poor, compromised solutions.

> 'Social, cultural, economic and ethnic inequalities are still being literally built into new places, with evidence showing that inclusive principles are not being adopted and implemented consistently. To address this, we need inclusive design thinking and practice to become core to the culture of the built environment industry.'
>
> Design Council[1]

Unfortunately, there are still many examples of buildings that have remained unchanged over the years, and of places that have been altered, improved or extended without inclusive design being part of the brief. As a result, many people still struggle to enjoy the services or activities that take place in these buildings.

Accessible elements are often value engineered out of a scheme during construction, with little or no understanding of the consequences for many disabled and older people, nor the additional costs and threat of possible legal redress that later alterations and adaptations of the built scheme entail.

But who are we designing for and why do we persist in labelling people and designing separate facilities for some sections of society? Shouldn't we all have the same experience when using our buildings, places and spaces? Who is 'disabled'? Aren't we all disabled in some way – by our environment, our attitudes, our life experiences, our financial circumstances? So why, when we design, construct and manage buildings and places, do we treat people so differently? Shouldn't the built environment be designed to be inclusive – designed to suit all our needs?

Impairment is normal, part of the human condition, something we all experience to a greater or lesser extent throughout our lives. Designs that ignore difference and diversity are ignoring ourselves, excluding the majority and denying the obvious.

My aim in this book is to put forward a powerful case for a change in attitude towards inclusivity and accessibility, considering the legal, social and moral arguments for inclusion and the business case (ignoring difference costs money – businesses are poorer, the economy and society lose out). More significantly, we cannot continue to discriminate against disabled and older people. We should accept that the system needs to change and that we should all be working hard to amend our behaviour and help create an industry that we can be proud of.

So, in Chapter 1 I go back in history, with a summary of how we got to where we are today – celebrating our achievements to date.

In Chapter 2 I look at the response of one local authority – the City of London Corporation – to the changes in planning and building legislation. A programme to improve access for disabled people has, over a period of 30 years, changed the City from a very inaccessible place to one where the streets and many of the buildings are much more welcoming.

Chapter 3 looks at how embracing diversity and inclusion from the very start of a major development project – the London 2012 Olympic and Paralympic Games – delivered the 'most accessible Games ever'. The chapter also considers the impact London 2012 had and continues to have on our attitude towards disabled people. It looks at whether the inclusive development process used to deliver the Games is changing our approach towards inclusive design and shifting attitudes and behaviours in the construction industry. Are clients and developers becoming champions of inclusion from the outset of their projects or are planning policy and building regulations still seen as the starting point of accessible design, not the regulatory safety net they are intended to be? By taking forward the Olympic Delivery Authority's successful inclusive development process and by going above and beyond minimum standards and regulations, the London Legacy Development Corporation (LLDC) is showing how to do it. The LLDC is creating, in the new developments in and around Queen Elizabeth Olympic Park, some of the most accessible and inclusive neighbourhoods in the UK.

Today there are some wonderful examples of new and refurbished buildings, including many historic listed buildings and ancient monuments, that disabled and older people can now use easily, safely and with dignity, alongside family and friends – good inclusive design that integrates all our access needs. This deserves to be celebrated, so Chapter 4 looks at some buildings and building elements that illustrate good inclusive design. As I have drawn on my own experience, most of the examples are from London, with some from elsewhere in England.

The devil is in the detail, however, and even in some generally very accessible places, opportunities to ensure everyone can use the building safely and easily are missed. The design of trains, buses, taxis and other forms of transport can, of course, have a major impact on our journeys, but I have concentrated on the built environment rather than on modes of transport (our journey towards making our public transport services accessible is a topic for another book!). It's not just the destination that needs to be accessible, but the journey from beginning to end. If any link in the journey access chain is broken between home and destination, the result can be failure to access the building or use the facility and hence exclusion. In the external environment this could be the lack of a dropped kerb or parking space, a step up into the bus from the bus stop or the lack of tactile paving on a train platform. An obstacle encountered on the footway, wide-open areas of paving with no guidance clues, poor signage and a lack of accessible seating and toilets can all make a journey stressful. When it comes to entering a building, problems can include the inability to identify the building entrance, a profusion of reflections and glare from large areas of glass at an entrance door, a locked 'accessible' entrance door, the lack of transitional lighting at the entrance, a remote and/or high reception desk, a noisy entrance lobby, induction loops out of order, the lack of clear signage, confusing wayfinding, narrow or heavy doors along corridors, a lift remote from the stairs or escalators and a lift out of order. Other issues include accessible toilets remote from the male and female provision, lack of seating and resting points, poor acoustics, highly patterned walls or shiny floor surfaces – the list goes on.

There is not enough space here to cover the full range of good and bad examples of an accessible built environment. (British Standard Code of Practice BS 8300:2018 provides a substantial amount of detail on all aspects of a building and the external environment and should be essential reading for all built environment professionals).[2] So, I finish Chapter 4 by looking at some common design pitfalls and some easy things to get right, including some good and bad examples of accessible public realm – the spaces between buildings – as well as some internal building elements.

Despite some excellent examples of accessible and inclusive buildings and places, we have not yet achieved our aim of an inclusive environment. Chapter 5 looks at whether the evolution of our legislation and regulations has hindered or constrained the achievement of an inclusive environment. We have a toolbox full of legislation, technical standards, guidance documents and years of experience, but we don't all use these tools effectively or learn from experience. I look at whether improvements to legislation, policy and regulations can accelerate change and how we can make better use of the tools we already have, and which need improving.

Chapter 6 looks at why, having made so much progress in recent years, inclusive design is still not fully embraced. Why is it still considered a 'have to do', rather than a 'good to do'? What are the barriers to inclusion and why does discrimination persist? I examine our attitude towards disabled people, our relationship with regulations and technical standards and why we still struggle to adopt the principles of inclusive design in our built environment projects. I consider what we can do to make access and inclusion second nature – business as usual – as basic as any other accepted 'normal' element of building design and construction. How can we value and build on the experience gained in the last 30 years? If we better integrate inclusive design into training and education programmes and improve our own knowledge, skills and understanding, we will know how to deliver inclusion from the start of our careers and be able to achieve it in all our future projects. I look at the business case for inclusive design and the growing awareness of the value of accessible buildings. With more than 13 million disabled people in the UK and more than a billion disabled people worldwide – a huge global market – the 'purple pound' can no longer be ignored. Coupled with the growing number of older people staying healthier and wealthier and wanting to continue living independent, active and dignified lives, the case for creating an inclusive environment is now indisputable. So how can architects and designers frame their discussions with clients? Access is not just a list of special features to be added to a final design, or just about wheelchair users or blind people – it's an attitude, a mind-set that embraces the full range of human difference.

We have not yet finished our journey from exclusion to inclusion – we still have some way to go before all our buildings, places and spaces are easy and comfortable for all of us to use. We all want to be able to lead dignified, independent and fulfilling lives, where unnecessary barriers and restrictions no longer hinder our opportunities. So, I conclude by asking what else we can do to ensure that we are not having these same debates in another 30 years. The key to success is surely to change our attitude and our behaviour and to make inclusive design an integral part of our normal, everyday built environment practice. I hope you find the book challenging and interesting, but most importantly I hope it helps you to believe that inclusive design is good for business, good for society, good for you and can no longer be ignored – and that **YOU** can be an inclusive designer.

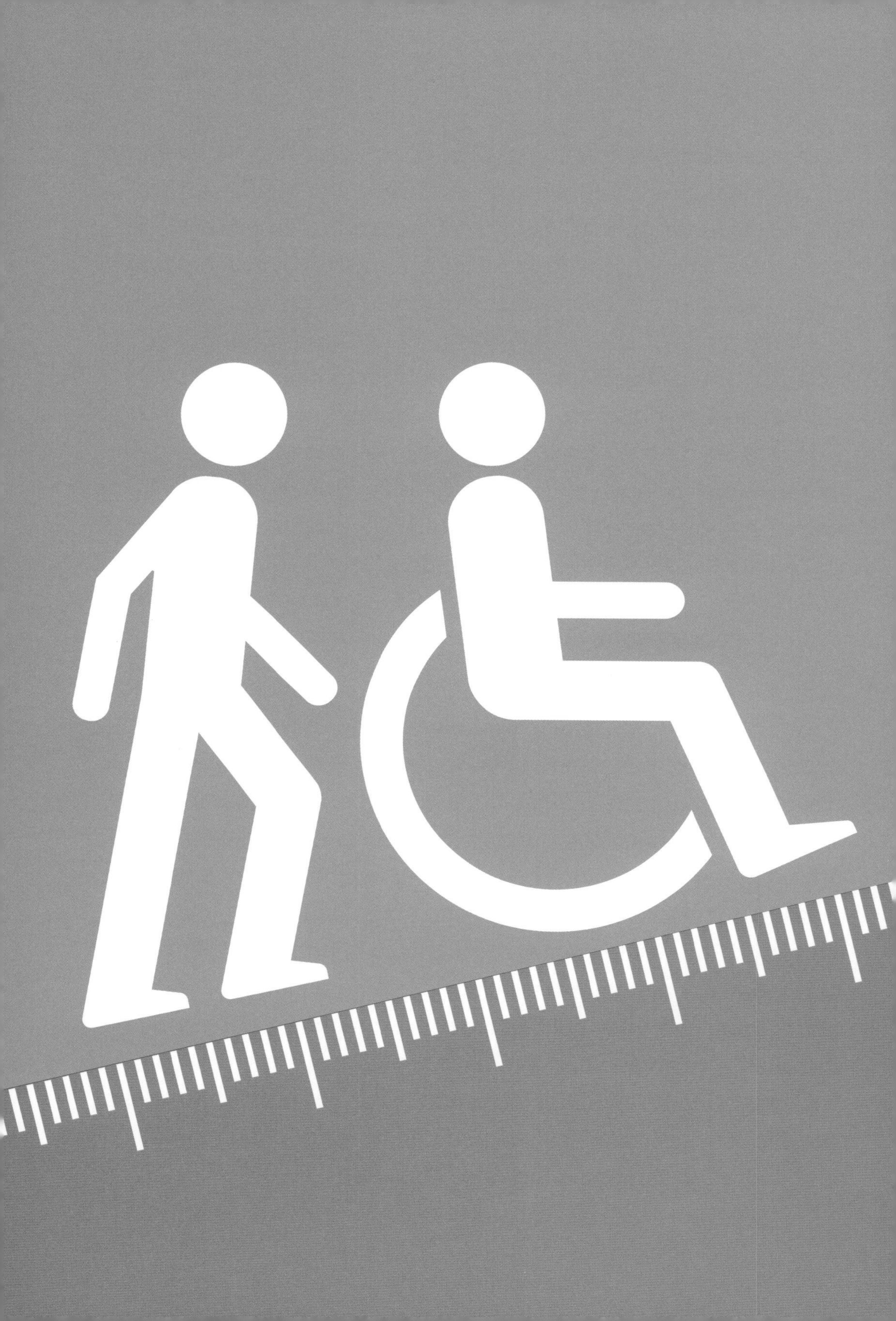

chapter **1**

How much have we achieved in 50 years?

'The challenges disabled people face in accessing homes, buildings and public spaces constitutes an unacceptable diminution of quality of life and equality.'

House of Commons Women and Equalities Committee, Building for Equality: Disability and the Built Environment, 2017[1]

In politics, in education and in our personal and professional lives, we like to feel we are more enlightened and inclusive than previous generations. But evidence presented to the House of Commons Women and Equalities Select Committee Inquiry into Disability and the Built Environment in 2016 heard that many disabled people still face difficulties accessing homes, buildings and public spaces.

Why is this when our knowledge and understanding about how to make buildings and places accessible is so much greater than it was when the first British Standard was published more than 50 years ago and the first building regulation requiring provision for disabled people in new buildings was introduced 30 years ago? Technical standards and building regulations have continued to improve and expand in their scope, and anti-discrimination legislation – the Disability Discrimination Act in 1995 and the Equality Act in 2010 – has ensured that access for disabled people has been firmly on the political agenda for more than 20 years.

Despite all this legislation, regulations, technical standards and years of experience, it is clear that we are still designing, building and maintaining architectural barriers that exclude a substantial proportion of our community. This chapter looks at what we have learnt about inclusive design since the first British Standard to address access for disabled people was published in 1967 – CP96 Access for the Disabled to Buildings[2] – and how technical standards, legislation and regulations have developed in the UK.

Half a century of technical standards

British Standard CP96 was influenced by the first technical standard produced in America in 1961[3] and the work undertaken by Selwyn Goldsmith in the first edition of his book 'Designing for the Disabled'[4] in 1963. It reflected the recognition that wheelchair users were excluded from society not as a result of their physical impairment or health condition but as a result of the lack of ramps, lifts, toilets and other facilities that enabled them to access and use a building. Selwyn Goldsmith, in his 1997 book The New Paradigm, eloquently describes this early history, providing a clear outline of how the first building standards were developed.[5]

It is interesting to look back at the very first access standard drafted in America in 1956 and the differences in approach taken at that time by the USA and the UK. Tim Nugent, manager of the rehabilitation education centre at the University of Illinois in Champaign-Urbana, wanted his disabled students to have the same education and be able to compete equally with non-disabled students. He did not want them to have to rely on welfare. The buildings within the university campus and the community facilities in the two local towns had, therefore, to be modified so that disabled students could use them independently. He developed an architectural brief to help remodel more than 200 university buildings and make them wheelchair accessible.

Nugent saw society as the origin of the problem for his disabled students. He explained:

> Physical and architectural barriers stand in the way of total rehabilitation. They stand between the disabled and their goals. They stand between the disabled and society. Many [disabled people] are afraid to venture forth because of the architectural barriers they encounter. We are basically concerned with making it possible for the great talents and resources of millions of physically disabled individuals to be put to use for the betterment of mankind by the elimination of architectural barriers.[6]

His pioneering work influenced the approach taken by the American Standards Association (which later became ANSI, the American National Standards Institute). Nugent conducted structured research with more than 400 disabled people and this data was used to inform the very first American national accessibility standard A117.1, published in 1961. These access standards – including the 1:12 ramp gradient – became very familiar and had a major influence on the development of access standards worldwide.

Design for special needs

In the UK the approach was not a macro/societal approach where barriers were to be removed so disabled people could participate on an equal basis, but one which Selwyn Goldsmith describes as the micro/welfare approach – whereby separate facilities are provided for disabled people rather than being integrated into mainstream facilities. This 'design for special needs' approach is well illustrated by the way accessible public toilet facilities are provided in the UK. Based on research Selwyn had undertaken with disabled people in Norwich, the first British Standard included a 'unisex' wheelchair-accessible WC designated specifically for use by disabled people. This gender-neutral WC enabled a wheelchair user to be accompanied by an assistant of the opposite sex without the embarrassment of entering the male or female toilets. This differed from the American approach, which advocated a wheelchair-accessible cubicle within the male and female WC provision.

It is interesting that there was even a debate about whether the solution should be the provision of special and separate facilities or designing mainstream facilities in a way that would also suit disabled people. The most inclusive solution is, of course, both. A wheelchair-accessible WC cubicle in the male and female provision integrates rather than segregates the independent user, while the separate unisex WC facility caters for those who need assistance from people of the opposite sex, as well as providing choice and flexibility for a wide variety of other users (many blind people use the unisex wheelchair-accessible WC as it has plenty of room for a guide dog). The UK regulations today do require a cubicle described as suitable for people with 'ambulant disabilities' integrated within the male and female provision, but it is too small for use by a wheelchair user, requiring all wheelchair users to queue for the only wheelchair-accessible facility available to them – the separate designated unisex WC. A larger wheelchair-accessible integrated cubicle would also provide more room for parents with small children.

The need for a variety of provision is clearly demonstrated today by the campaign to install Changing Places WCs in large public buildings, in addition to the standard unisex wheelchair-accessible WC required by regulation. Designed for use by people with complex and multiple impairments who need assistance, the room includes a peninsula toilet and basin, an adult-sized changing bench, a hoist and an optional shower (Figure 1.1). Without these specially designed and equipped facilities, over a quarter of a million people who need Changing Places toilets could not get out and about and enjoy the day-to-day activities many of us take for granted.[7] This is now recognised by the government, which is consulting on a change to Part M of the building regulations to make Changing Places toilets mandatory in new large public buildings such as shopping centres and cinemas, and has announced an investment of £2 million to enable the National Health Service (NHS) to install more than 100 Changing Places toilets in NHS hospitals.[8] This follows a £2 million investment by the Department for Transport to increase the number of Changing Places toilets in motorway service stations.

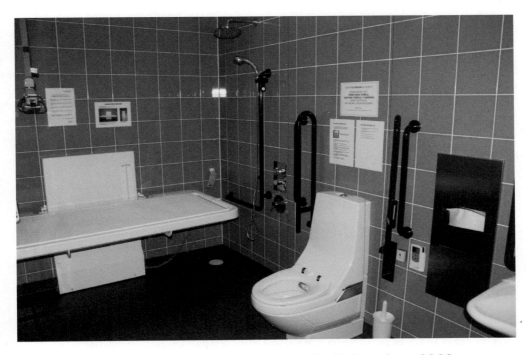

Figure 1.1 **Changing Places toilet, City Hall, London, 2008: an existing (inaccessible) toilet and shower room on the ground floor of City Hall was converted by Ann Sawyer, of Access=Design, into a 'Changing Places' toilet.**

The standard (inaccessible) WC provision today is increasingly unisex, recognising diversity and difference in users – non-gender labelling makes it easier for transgender people to use. By incorporating the wash-hand basin within the cubicle, these slightly larger cubicles are easier for everyone to use, particularly women, who have had to put up with tiny toilet cubicles for years.

Choice, flexibility and a variety of both integrated provision (inclusive design) and separate provision (accessible design that meets a particular need) should be the aim, especially in larger buildings and public places.

The first legislation to address access to buildings

Today, the first American standard and the first British standard seem very limited in their scope, in their application and in the dimensions used, but they were, in both countries, the catalyst to effecting significant legislative change.

In 1969 Jack Ashley MP established the All-Party Disablement Group and, having won the ballot that year to introduce a private members' bill, he successfully steered the 1970 Chronically Sick and Disabled Persons Act (CSDP Act) onto the statute book.

Section 4 of the CSDP Act placed a duty on anyone providing a public building to make provision for disabled people in terms of access into and within the building, and for parking and sanitary facilities. The application of these requirements was, however, very limited – provision was required only 'in so far as it is in the circumstances both practicable and reasonable' and only in public buildings. Many local authorities did, however, start to make improvements to their public buildings, but as the government did not introduce the necessary regulations to enforce Section 4, there was no way of enforcing provision, so many other public buildings remained inaccessible. Employment buildings were not included – presumably on the assumption that disabled people did not work.

As well as introducing a range of special services for disabled people, the Act required local housing authorities to have regard to the 'special needs' of disabled people in relation to the provision of new housing. This led to the development in the 1970s of technical advice on the design of accessible housing. The government published advice on the design of mobility homes in 1974[9] (the forerunner of Lifetime Homes) and wheelchair accessible homes in 1975,[10] so it is staggering that more than 40 years later we are still not, as a matter of course, building mainstream housing that fully integrates these basic accessibility standards.

It is, however, fascinating to look back to 1993 and the direction the government was moving in with regard to the need to build more homes accessible to disabled people. Government planning policy in 1993 included, in Planning Policy Guidance 3: Housing (PPG 3), that a local authority development policy on accessible housing may be appropriate where there is clear evidence of local need. The limitations of the UK building regulations were being recognised and consideration was being given to making access to housing a requirement of the building regulations. Despite the optimism in 1993, the Joseph Rowntree Foundation and the Access Committee for England, along with numerous organisations of disabled people who campaigned for Lifetime Homes throughout the 1990s, had to wait until 1999 to see the start of a change in housing design. The first very limited provisions introduced into the building regulations were aimed at enabling new homes to be visited by disabled people. Provisions included a level or ramped approach, a level entrance, a wide front door with generous internal circulation, a downstairs WC (which was not required to be wheelchair accessible) and switches and socket outlets at a reachable height. But even this caused a storm in the press when the cry went up that the traditional doorstep was being lost! It took another 16 years before the building regulations were amended to incorporate accessible housing standards, but even these standards are optional. The building regulations were substantially improved in 2015 to finally include the Lifetime Home standards (with slight variations) and wheelchair-accessible standards (see Part M, Volume 1, M4(2) and M4(3)).[11] However, adoption of these standards is dependent on the local planning authority addressing the need for accessible housing in its local plan and including explicit policies on their implementation, and unfortunately, many local planning authorities still lack such policies (see Chapter 5 for further discussion on this).

The social model of disability

Despite the limitations of the 1970 CSDP Act, it did begin to raise the profile of accessible design within the architectural profession. But change was very slow and disabled people were starting to raise their voices collectively and disruptively, eventually resulting in a very active Disability Movement. In 1976, the Union of the Physically Impaired Against Segregation (UPIAS) stated:

In our view it is society which disables physically impaired people. Disability is something imposed on top of our impairments by the way we are unnecessarily isolated and excluded from full participation in society. Disabled people are therefore an oppressed group in society. It follows from this analysis that having low incomes, for example, is only one aspect of our oppression. It is a consequence of our isolation and segregation, in every area of life, such as education, work, mobility, housing, etc. Poverty is one symptom of our oppression, but it is not the cause.[12]

This initiated the social model of disability – a practical tool for effecting social and political change – first used by academic and disability rights activist Mike Oliver in 1983 and still used today.[13] The social model places the responsibility for change on society, not on the individual disabled person. The way society responds to disabled people is the main cause of social exclusion – disability is created by barriers in society, by people's attitude (stereotyping, discrimination and prejudice), environmental barriers (inaccessible buildings and services) and organisations (inflexible policies, practices and procedures). The social model enabled disparate groups and individuals to work together for change. Organisations of disabled people grew in number and strength during the 1980s and 1990s, many with a specific focus on tackling the lack of access to buildings and transport.

The Access Committee for England

The Access Committee for England (ACE) was launched in 1984 as a subcommittee of the Centre on Environment for the Handicapped (a charity established in 1969 to promote better access for disabled people, called since 1990 the Centre for Accessible Environments). The committee was made up of regulators (local authority planning and building control officers, and fire officers), users (organisations of disabled people and local access groups) and providers (architects, developers and building owners). The need to reach a consensus in any discussion provided a strength and dynamism to the committee's work.

In 1991 ACE supported the launch of the Access Association – a network of local authority access officers which has now expanded its membership beyond local government to include access consultants and others in the private sector involved in improving access for disabled people. There was a debate at the time about whether ACE should also launch and support a network of local access groups. By the mid-1990s there were more than 400 groups, and many were struggling to get their voices heard – they wanted to engage and participate in the planning system and help local planning authorities use their power and influence to improve access. However, ACE had decided against supporting the launch of a national network of access groups, a decision which in retrospect may have made it harder for many local access groups to survive local government funding cuts.

The first planning policies

In 1979 CP96 was withdrawn and replaced by British Standard BS 5810 Code of Practice for Access for the Disabled to Buildings (by 2001 it became the now familiar BS 8300).[14] The access issue was clearly highlighted to government in a 1979 report titled Can Disabled People Go Where You Go?[15] This report, produced by the Silver Jubilee Committee on Improving Access for Disabled People, which was set up in 1977 by Alf Morris MP and chaired by Sir Peter Large (who went on to chair CORAD, the Committee on Restrictions Against Disabled People), made a number of recommendations. One of these was that local authorities should appoint access officers as a point of contact for disabled people and to help advise planning officers when granting planning permission. This led to the introduction, in the 1981 Disabled Persons Act, of further legislative duties regarding access for disabled people.

It seemed like a major step forward when access for disabled people became a planning matter and the government introduced the first planning policies. The 1981 Disabled Persons Act introduced Section 29A and Section 29B into the 1971 Town and Country Planning Act. This placed a duty on local planning authorities, on the grant of planning permission, to draw the attention of developers to the provisions of the Chronically Sick and Disabled Persons Act 1970 and to BS 5810:1979. Means of access, parking and sanitary conveniences were to be provided in certain types of building where reasonable and practicable.

By 1982 the government had interpreted these duties in a Development Control Policy Note, setting out how planning authorities should be addressing access for disabled people and recommending the appointment of access officers. This stimulated activity throughout the 1980s. The first local authority access officer was appointed by Leicester City Council, and many other councils followed, including the Corporation of London (which appointed its first access officer early in 1988). Some councils, such as Wandsworth Borough Council, took the view that all staff should be aware of the issues, so they did not appoint a specific member of staff as an access officer, but tagged the duties onto the job functions of a senior planner.

Following the intervention of Wandsworth Disablement Association, which challenged Wandsworth Council Planning Department to do more to improve access for disabled people in the borough, as senior planner I was asked to draft a planning policy and design guidelines on access for disabled people. As a result, the 1988 Wandsworth Borough Plan included the following policy:

Access and facilities for people with disabilities should be provided in all new developments and in existing buildings undergoing major extensions and adaptations, in accordance with the Council's Access Design Guidelines. The external environment including parking areas and areas of open space should also be designed to provide access for people with disabilities in accordance with these guidelines. Where access and facilities already exist the level of provision should be maintained or improved, not reduced.[16]

By 1993 the Royal Town Planning Institute (RTPI) had published a package of access policies giving advice for all planning authorities. The introduction recognised that 'people with disabilities are precluded from playing a full and independent role in society by the inaccessibility of land, buildings, transport and other facilities in the environment'.[17] The RTPI drew on the advice provided by the government in its Planning Policy Guidance 1: General Policy and Principles (PPG1), published in March 1992[18] – which stressed the opportunity created by the development of land and buildings to secure a more accessible environment and the importance of considering access at an early stage in the design process. The RTPI's model planning policies included an overarching strategy statement, policies on access to commercial and residential buildings, residential care, highways and transport, shopping, leisure and tourism and access to the countryside – a comprehensive set of policies which local authorities could easily adopt or adapt as appropriate to their local area and incorporate into their borough plans (Figure 1.2). It is disappointing that today, more than 25 years later, there are still many planning authorities which have not embedded inclusive design policies into their local plans.

Figure 1.2 Over the last 30 years, there has been an expanding toolbox of policies, regulations, technical standards and advice regarding accessibility, including the following:

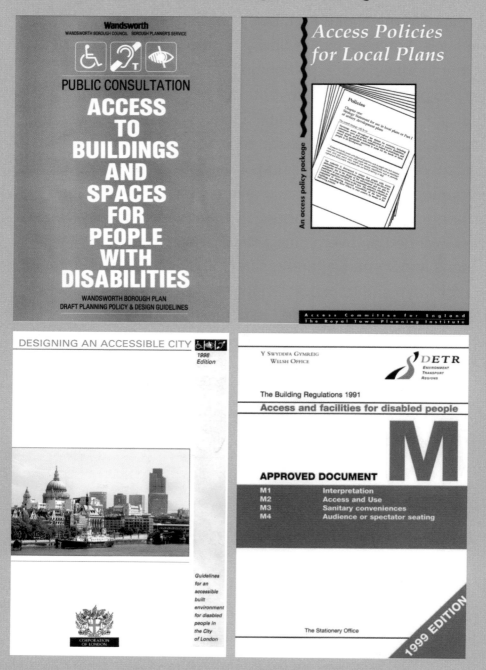

Supplementary Planning Guidance

Accessible London: achieving an inclusive environment
The London Plan Supplementary Planning Guidance

April 2004

MAYOR OF LONDON

The principles of inclusive design.
(They include you.)

CABE

**SHAPING NEIGHBOURHOODS
ACCESSIBLE LONDON: ACHIEVING AN
INCLUSIVE ENVIRONMENT**
SUPPLEMENTARY PLANNING GUIDANCE

OCTOBER 2014

LONDON PLAN 2011
IMPLEMENTATION FRAMEWORK　MAYOR OF LONDON

BS 8300-2:2018

BSI Standards Publication

**Design of an accessible and inclusive
built environment**

Part 2: Buildings — Code of practice

bsi.

Design and Access Statements

An interesting shift took place in government policy with the introduction of the Planning and Compulsory Purchase Act in 2004. The 1990 Town and Country Planning Act was repealed, including Section 76 (previously sections 29A and 29B of the 1971 Act), which had placed a legal duty on planning authorities to draw the attention of developers to the access needs of disabled people. The need to introduce a new statutory duty on local authorities was raised with Tony McNulty MP, Parliamentary Under Secretary of State at the Office of the Deputy Prime Minister, at an RTPI conference on the Planning and Compulsory Purchase Bill in March 2003. His view was that the way forward was to take 'the thrust of Section 76 throughout the new planning system to ensure that developers should be alerted to disability access legislation at the earliest opportunity in the planning process'.[19] The new Act (after a successful amendment was made as the bill was going through Parliament) introduced the requirement for planning applications to be accompanied by 'a statement about the design principles and concepts that have been applied to the development and how issues relating to access to the development had been dealt with'. The subsequent General Development Order made it clear that the Design and Access Statement should cover both design and access, 'allowing applicants to demonstrate an integrated approach that will deliver inclusive design and address a full range of access requirements throughout the design process'.[20] The Commission for Architecture and the Built Environment (CABE) published guidance on Design and Access Statements in 2006 and this became a well-used tool to assist planning officers when considering a planning application.[21]

Policy appeared to be strengthened when PPG 1 was replaced
in 2005 by Planning Policy Statement 1, which stressed the
fundamental role good design plays in achieving the delivery of
sustainable development and stated: 'Good design is indivisible
from good planning. Planning authorities should plan positively
for the achievement of high quality and inclusive design in all
development, including in individual buildings, public and private
spaces and wider development area schemes'.[22] This approach
was clearly articulated in the foreword to a good practice guide
on planning and access for disabled people published by the
Office of the Deputy Prime Minister in March 2003:

> The Government is fully committed to an inclusive society
> in which nobody is disadvantaged. An important part of
> delivering this commitment is breaking down unnecessary
> physical barriers and exclusions imposed on disabled
> people by poor design of buildings and places. Too often
> the needs of disabled people are considered late in the
> day and separately from the needs of others. We want
> to change that. We want the needs of disabled people
> properly considered as an integral part of the development
> process. As our July 2002 document Sustainable
> Communities: Delivering Through Planning made clear, the
> land use planning system has a key role to play in creating
> and sustaining mixed and inclusive communities.[23]

As well as encouraging local planning authorities to have
comprehensive planning policies in their development plan,
raise inclusive access issues at pre-application meetings
and use the expertise of access officers and local access

groups to help assess the effectiveness of provision, the guide encouraged the submission of access statements with a planning application. The aim was to encourage the developer to demonstrate their commitment to inclusive design at the earliest stage in the process and for the designer to clearly identify in the planning application the philosophy and approach taken to deliver inclusive access. The government recognised that many places remained inaccessible to disabled people and this was, in part, due to many schemes being given planning consent without anyone properly assessing the accessibility of the proposal. Developers as well as designers were encouraged to understand the importance of delivering an inclusive environment and to integrate the needs of all potential users of the scheme from the outset.

Despite this policy advice, I often reflect on whether removing Section 76 from the Planning Act had a detrimental effect on whether and how some planning authorities addressed access and inclusive design issues, with some pushing it further into the building regulation arena despite the intention of making it an issue to address at the beginning of the development process.

The London Plan

The creation in 2000 of the new strategic authority in London – the Greater London Authority (GLA) – did, however, provide an opportunity to demonstrate and implement robust inclusive design planning policies. The GLA used government planning policy advice when drafting policies for the first London Plan, published in 2004. A range of policies addressing the access needs of

The London Plan 2004

Spatial Development Strategy for Greater London

Policy 4B.5 Creating an inclusive environment

The Mayor of London will require all future development to meet the highest standards of accessibility and inclusion.

Unitary Development Plan policies should integrate and adopt the following principles of inclusive design that will require that developments:

- can be used easily by as many people as possible without undue effort, separation, or special treatment

- offer the freedom to choose and the ability to participate equally in the development's mainstream activities

- value diversity and difference

Boroughs should require development proposals to include an Access Statement showing how the principles of inclusive design, including the specific needs of disabled people, have been integrated into the proposed development, and how inclusion will be maintained and managed.

These principles and the requirements of Policy 3A.14 'Addressing the needs of London's diverse population' should be adopted by all responsible for changing or managing the built environment.[24]

disabled people were included throughout the plan, guided by an overarching policy, Policy 4B.5, requiring the highest standards of access and inclusion in all development proposals.

Supplementary planning guidance titled 'Accessible London: Achieving an Inclusive Environment' was published by the GLA in 2004, providing detailed advice on how to meet the London Plan policies (Figure 1.3).[25]

Figure 1.3 **Mayor of London Ken Livingstone launches the draft Supplementary Planning Guidance Accessible London for public consultation in 2003; from left to right: Caroline Gooding (disability advisor to the Mayor of London's cabinet), Peter Barker (Visiting Professor in Inclusive Environments at The University of Reading), Ken Livingstone and the author.**

London continues to demonstrate that embracing inclusive design in a strategic plan can be very effective. The London Plan has now been replaced by its third incarnation. All three versions (Ken Livingstone's in 2004, Boris Johnson's in 2011 and Sadiq Khan's draft London Plan, published for consultation in December 2017) include very similar inclusive design policies.

Khan's draft plan not only includes a similar key policy on inclusive design (Policy D3) but also 'Building strong and inclusive communities' is the first of six 'Good Growth Policies' that form the backbone of the plan. The principles of inclusive design are set out in the very first policy – Plan Policy GG1.

The London Plan: Draft for Public Consultation, December 2017

Policy GG1 Building strong and inclusive communities

To build on the city's tradition of openness, diversity and equality, and help deliver strong and inclusive communities, those involved in planning and development must ...

- support the creation of a London where all Londoners, including older people, disabled people and people with young children, can move around with ease and enjoy the opportunities the city provides, creating a welcoming environment that everyone can use confidently, independently and with choice and dignity, avoiding separation or segregation.[26]

This is reinforced in the design chapter, where Policy D3 on inclusive design articulates the principles in more detail.

The London Plan: Draft for Public Consultation, December 2017

Policy D3 Inclusive design

A To deliver an inclusive environment and meet the needs of all Londoners, development proposals are required to achieve the highest standards of accessible and inclusive design, ensuring they:

1. can be entered and used safely, easily and with dignity by all

2. are convenient and welcoming with no disabling barriers, providing independent access without additional undue effort, separation or special treatment

3. are designed to incorporate safe and dignified emergency evacuation for all building users. In developments where lifts are installed, as a minimum at least one lift per core (or more subject to capacity assessments) should be a fire evacuation lift suitable to be used to evacuate people who require level access from the building.

B The Design and Access Statement, submitted as part of planning applications, should include an inclusive design statement.[27]

The draft London Plan has undergone an extensive public consultation process and an amendment to supporting paragraph 3.3.1 has been suggested to clarify the policy:

It is essential to consider inclusive design at the earliest possible stage in a scheme's development, and inclusive design should be embedded into a project from initial conception through to completion, occupation and in the on-going management and maintenance of the development. Master plans and design codes should therefore embed and document the highest standards of inclusive design, for this approach to be carried forward throughout the development of projects.[28]

Using inclusive design expertise will help developers and applicants get it right from the outset. This is reinforced in another amendment to the draft London Plan – in the supporting text to Policy D3 (paragraph 3.3.7A):

The planning of inclusive design elements of development proposals and the drafting of inclusive design statements should be undertaken by or have input from a suitably qualified specialist with relevant experience in inclusive design, such as a member of the National Register of Access Consultants. Local authority access officers or inclusive design advisors should assist in the evaluation of development proposals and inclusive design statements in terms of inclusive design.[29]

The plan is, at the time of writing, going through an Examination in Public before it can be published as the adopted plan (expected to happen at some point before the next mayoral elections in May 2020), but I am confident that the inclusive design policies will remain virtually unchanged. The key to success is how well the policies are implemented by the boroughs and by the Mayor of London when he considers the strategic planning applications referred to him. Good enforcement is key to the success of any planning policy. However, despite good intentions, inclusive design policies are not always enforced as robustly as they should be, with some boroughs excelling in this area and others not performing quite so well. It remains to be seen how well the boroughs respond to the policies in the new London Plan and whether the policies are comprehensively enforced. Support for accessible and inclusive design by the Planning Inspectorate when dealing with borough plan inquiries and planning appeals is also an essential part of the enforcement jigsaw. Chapter 5 discusses some of the barriers to enforcement.

The first building regulation

In the 1980s it was very frustrating that planning legislation was limited to raising access issues 'on the grant of planning permission'. It seemed a missed opportunity not to be able to negotiate good accessibility as part of the planning process – raising the issue as an informative on the grant of planning permission was far too late. However, the introduction into the 1985 Building Regulations of 'Access and Facilities in Buildings for the Benefit of Disabled People' (Part T, which became Approved Document M in 1987) was a turning point in the provision of facilities for disabled people, albeit it took another 30 years before the regulations became anywhere near comprehensive. The 1987 provisions were very limited in their scope, addressing only the physical features that would assist wheelchair users and disabled people with walking impairments and applicable only in very limited circumstances. Part M required that reasonable provision was made for disabled people to gain access to certain (commercial) buildings, and to sanitary facilities and audience and spectator seating, where provided. The only buildings covered by the regulations were new shops and offices, the principal entrance storey of new factories, schools and other educational establishments, and premises where the public were admitted. It did, however, state that where an existing building was extended or materially altered, access and facilities for disabled people should be maintained. It wasn't until a revision in 1991 that design considerations for blind and partially sighted people and people with hearing loss were addressed, and it was 1999 before Part M applied to all commercial buildings.

Selwyn Goldsmith outlines an interesting debate at the time between the welfare approach introduced by the new regulation of designing special and separate facilities for disabled people and the alternative approach of designing for everyone. Patrick Jenkin, Secretary of State for the Environment in 1985, is quoted by Selwyn as saying that the new regulation would give disabled people the opportunity 'to contribute, to make choices, to seek new horizons, to realise their potential'.

The aim was to guide those who design, construct and manage public buildings, but Jenkin recognised that to create accessible environments there had to be collaboration from planners, developers, architects, building control officers, building managers and fire officers, along with representatives of disabled people. He also wanted a shift in attitude away from a focus on the individual, towards what we would recognise today as an inclusive approach, asking:

> Ought we constantly to treat disabled people as a special group, as disadvantaged people with special problems, who need special attention and special amenities and special gadgetry?
>
> Isn't the best way, wherever we can, to make all our buildings accessible to everyone – so that they cater, as a matter of course, equally for those who are disabled as well as for those who are able-bodied?[30]

Another interesting comment at that time was that setting out technical design data which highlights special requirements 'tends to make us forget whatever designing for the disabled has in common with designing for anyone else'.[31] Despite the immense progress made in the last 30 years, we are still stuck in this 'design for special needs' philosophy that confuses and thus avoids the need to create an inclusive environment – one that caters for 'special needs' as well as an environment that integrates and accommodates independent and dignified inclusive access for a diversity of people, not a homogenous group of 'disabled people'.

The principles of inclusive design

A further change in approach was taking place throughout the 1990s. The limitations of the UK Building Regulations were recognised, and they were revised in 1991 to include some provisions to assist blind and partially sighted people and people with hearing loss. Bert Massie, Chair of RADAR (the Royal Association of Disability and Rehabilitation) always complained that it was his whiskey his neighbours drank every Christmas as he was unable to access his neighbours' homes in his wheelchair. He had to wait until 1999 to see the start of a change in housing design when the first very limited provisions to enable new homes to be visited by disabled people were introduced.

In America, Ron Mace, a disabled architect and accessibility law expert, recognised the need for a different approach and started using the term Universal Design. He collaborated with a group of architects, product designers, engineers and environmental design researchers, and established the following Principles of Universal Design to help guide a wide range of design disciplines, including environments, products and communications:

1. equitable use

2. flexibility in use

3. simple and intuitive use

4. perceptible information

5. tolerance for error

6. low physical effort

7. size and space for approach and use[32]

This concept moved away from the rehabilitation model and designing specifically for disabled people and instead was aimed at 'designing products and environments to be useable by all people, to the greatest extent possible, without the need for adaptation or specialised design'.[33]

A similar process was taking place in the UK. Roger Coleman (co-founder and co-director of the Helen Hamlyn Research Centre from 1999 until 2008 and now Professor Emeritus of the Royal College of Art) wrote extensively on inclusive design and worked closely with Professor John Clarkson, director of the Engineering Design Centre at Cambridge University, to develop inclusive design tools and guidance for industry.[34] The inclusive design concept was also being applied to the built environment and discussions at the Centre for Accessible Environments, the Disability Rights Commission's Built Environment Reference Group and the Disabled Persons Transport Advisory Committee's Built Environment Working Group developed the UK's approach to an inclusive built environment. When responsibility for advising government on inclusive design and access issues was passed to CABE in 1999, CABE's Inclusive Environment Group agreed the following:

- Inclusive design is about making places everyone can use.
- Inclusive design is everyone's responsibility.
- Good design is inclusive design.

A definition of the Principles of Inclusive Design, which is still being used today, was published by CABE in 2006 in 'The Principles of Inclusive Design (They include you)'.

The Principles of Inclusive Design

1. Inclusive design places people at the heart of the design process.
2. Inclusive design acknowledges diversity and difference.
3. Inclusive design offers choice where a single design solution cannot accommodate all users.
4. Inclusive design provides for flexibility in use.
5. Inclusive design provides buildings and environments that are convenient and enjoyable to use for everyone.

If you follow the five principles of inclusive design, you should end up with [developments that are]:

- inclusive so everyone can use them safely, easily and with dignity
- responsive, taking account of what people say they need and want
- flexible, so different people can use them in different ways
- convenient, so everyone can use them without too much effort or separation
- accommodating for all people, regardless of their age, gender, mobility, ethnicity or circumstances
- welcoming, with no disabling barriers that might exclude some people
- realistic, offering more than one solution to help balance everyone's needs and recognising that one solution may not work for all.[35]

Moving away from specific designs for disabled people towards the inclusive design concept was also addressed in the 2004 edition of Part M of the Building Regulations. Significantly, it was no longer called 'Access and facilities for disabled people' but became 'Access to and use of buildings', recognising that the standards it recommended were of benefit to everyone, not just disabled people, helping to integrate access needs into mainstream provision – an inclusive design approach. More changes to Part M followed in 2010, 2013 and 2015, with calls to improve it again following the publication by the British Standards Institution in January 2018 of the revised and updated code of practice BS 8300:2018 Design of an accessible and inclusive built environment.[36]

Divided into two parts – Part One on the external environment and Part Two covering buildings – BS 8300:2018 is probably the most comprehensive technical guide to creating an inclusive environment that exists anywhere in the world at this moment in time. The BSI committee with responsibility for BS 8300 does, however, recognise that further knowledge and expertise is needed about facilities that address neurological requirements and supports the current BSI work programme looking at these issues. The Helen Hamlyn Centre for Design at the Royal College of Art has been undertaking research on behalf of BSI, exploring how to improve and tailor the built environment to consider the needs of people living with dementia, autism, dyslexia, dyspraxia and a range of other neurological diversities. BSI is now considering publishing a PAS (Publicly Accessible Standard) called 'Design for the Mind'.[37] Technical standards will continue to improve as we further develop and improve our knowledge and understanding.

Despite the comprehensive advice in the British Standard and in the building regulations, common design pitfalls are still frequently seen in new and refurbished buildings – Chapter 4 looks at several. This begs the question of how many planners, architects and designers know, read and use BS 8300 and whether technical standards are all we need to ensure that everyone has the same ability to access and use our buildings. Chapter 4 looks at several common design pitfalls still seen in new and refurbished buildings despite the advice in the British Standard and in the Building Regulations.

Civil rights legislation

Despite the improvements in planning policy and building regulations during the 1990s, further legislation was needed to enforce the standards and to help create a more accessible environment, and more importantly to give disabled people themselves the power to shape and influence the design of the environment. The introduction in 1995 of the Disability Discrimination Act (DDA) and the requirement by 2004 of service providers to anticipate user needs, make reasonable adjustments and, in certain circumstances, make their buildings accessible, was a huge incentive to both employers and building providers. The end of the 1990s and the beginning of the 2000s saw a rise in awareness and a developing anxiety about meeting the legislative requirements of the DDA. Fearing legal redress if they ignored the Act, many building owners finally started to consider the physical accessibility of their buildings and commissioned access audits in advance of the 2004 requirements and assessed what improvements they could undertake to ensure equal, safe and dignified access for disabled people.

As the DDA was going through Parliament, the government
recognised that disabled people would need help and advice if
they were to successfully take cases of discrimination through
the courts and suggested that the Access Committee for England
could run a helpline. But with only two permanent members of
staff, that was not going to work. So there was great relief when
the Disability Advisory Service was set up and, in December
1997, the Disability Rights Task Force was established. The Task
Force's remit was to advise the government how best to deliver
on the commitment to comprehensive and enforceable civil rights
for disabled people. The Disability Rights Task Force report From
Exclusion to Inclusion, published in 1999, commented in its
introduction that:

Attitudes to disabled people have changed
significantly. From seeing disabled people as the
passive recipients of charity, society has come
to recognise the legitimate demands for disabled
people to have equal rights. However, traditional
preconceptions and long held prejudices still prevail.
Barriers that prevent full participation in society
confront disabled people every day of their lives.
Activities that the rest of society takes for granted
are denied to many disabled people.[38]

This led to the establishment in April 2000 of the Disability
Rights Commission (DRC), which through its website and
comprehensive helpline assisted disabled people to secure their
rights under the DDA. It provided an independent conciliation
service in the event of disputes between disabled people

and service providers and had powers to undertake formal investigations into how disabled people were treated by an organisation, and into unlawful acts by an organisation.

As well as running a comprehensive helpline, the DRC, through the work of its Built Environment Reference Group and legal team, published a plethora of codes of practice, providing advice to employers and service providers, spelling out what could be considered reasonable provision and how to ensure they were not being discriminatory. Exemplary accessibility was clearly demonstrated in the DRC's own offices in London – once inside the building there were wide automatic doors with large colour-contrasting push plates, generous access routes and ample space between desks for wheelchair users to turn easily and for guide dogs to rest. The atmosphere was intense and dynamic, with a very forward-looking and enthusiastic team who recognised the difference they were making to the lives of disabled people. The team was, however, sadly disbanded when the DRC was absorbed into the Equality and Human Rights Commission in 2007.

The Centre for Accessible Environments (CAE) was kept busy during this period, advising businesses on how to meet their obligations under the Act. One useful, inexpensive service it provided to small businesses was a walk-and-talk survey – during a consultation lasting an hour or two, the owner of a small shop could be advised how to improve access in a sensible and practical way. Access consultants were also kept busy undertaking more comprehensive access audits and several books and guidance documents were published advising what to assess and how to manage the task.[39] To regulate the work of access consultants, the government supported CAE in a project to set up the National Register of Access Consultants (NRAC), an independent UK-wide accreditation service whose members have been providing independent access and inclusive design advice since 1999.[40]

Access consultants today, however, report that demand for access auditing work has diminished – they undertake far fewer access audits now than previously, yet you still see many premises that have obviously not fully considered the needs of their disabled customers. Austerity measures mean that local authorities have fewer resources to appoint specialist access advisors and discrimination cases rarely reach the courts due to the reduction in the availability of legal aid. If a restaurant or pub does not have an accessible toilet, instead of taking a case under the Equality Act most people will just go to another pub that does provide the facilities. Businesses lose out when they don't provide for disabled customers. (See Chapter Six for further discussion on this.)

We still have a long way to go to achieve inclusion

This chapter has illustrated our journey from the first very limited technical standards introduced in the 1960s, to the gradual introduction over the next 50 years of planning, building and equality legislation and regulations (Figure 1.4, overleaf). The UK, rightly, now has a worldwide reputation for its excellent anti-discrimination legislation, regulations and technical standards. With this history it should, by now, be second nature to build, manage and maintain our buildings in a way that fully integrates everyone's needs. It's not just wheelchair users and blind people – the two 'impairments' specified in the very first building regulation, but whatever your disability, age or health condition, you should not be encountering physical barriers in the built environment. Yet many disabled and older people still find it difficult to access homes, jobs, shops and leisure facilities.

Chapter 5 looks at why, despite considerable improvements in the accessibility of our built environment, our legislation and government policy has failed to deliver an inclusive environment for all, and Chapter 6 discusses whether prevailing traditional preconceptions and long-held prejudices are the key to this failure. On a more positive note, Chapter 2 looks at how one local authority – the City of London Corporation – responded to the legislative and regulatory changes introduced in the 1980s and 1990s and developed an awareness of the need to make its streets and buildings more accessible – an approach that still has relevance today.

Key

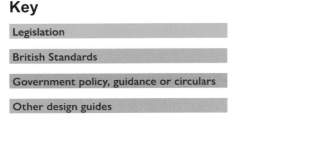

Legislation

British Standards

Government policy, guidance or circulars

Other design guides

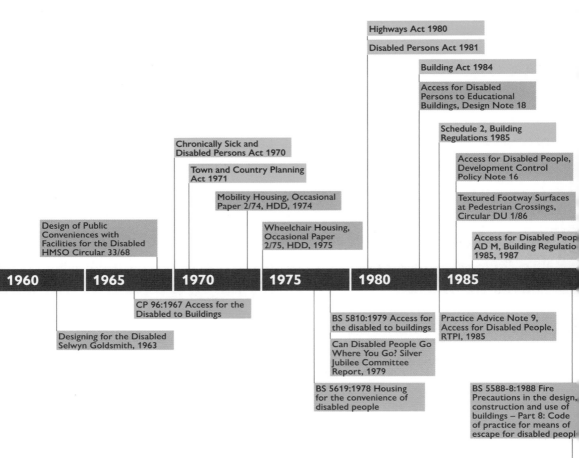

Highways Act 1980

Disabled Persons Act 1981

Building Act 1984

Access for Disabled Persons to Educational Buildings, Design Note 18

Schedule 2, Building Regulations 1985

Access for Disabled People, Development Control Policy Note 16

Textured Footway Surfaces at Pedestrian Crossings, Circular DU 1/86

Access for Disabled People AD M, Building Regulatio 1985, 1987

Chronically Sick and Disabled Persons Act 1970

Town and Country Planning Act 1971

Mobility Housing, Occasional Paper 2/74, HDD, 1974

Wheelchair Housing, Occasional Paper 2/75, HDD, 1975

Design of Public Conveniences with Facilities for the Disabled HMSO Circular 33/68

1960   1965   1970   1975   1980   1985

CP 96:1967 Access for the Disabled to Buildings

BS 5810:1979 Access for the disabled to buildings

Practice Advice Note 9, Access for Disabled People, RTPI, 1985

Designing for the Disabled Selwyn Goldsmith, 1963

Can Disabled People Go Where You Go? Silver Jubilee Committee Report, 1979

BS 5619:1978 Housing for the convenience of disabled people

BS 5588-8:1988 Fire Precautions in the design, construction and use of buildings – Part 8: Code of practice for means of escape for disabled peopl

Good Loo Design Guide, Centre on Environment fe the Handicapped, 1988

Figure 1.4 **Timeline of legislation, regulations and technical standards**

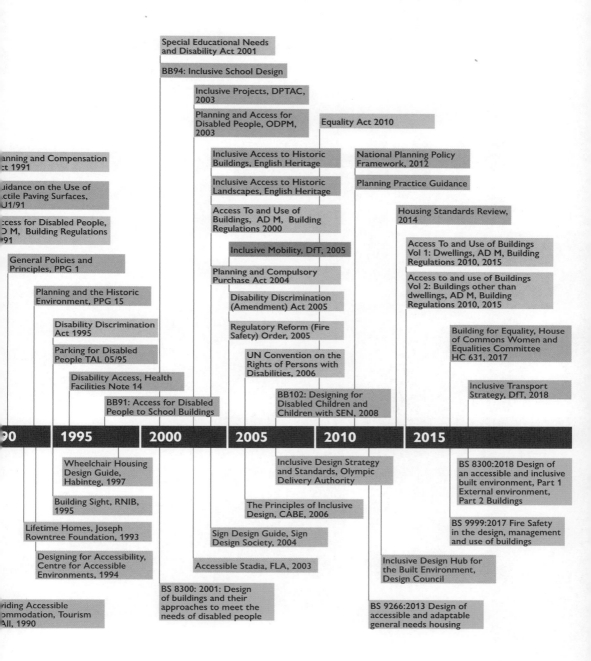

chapter **2**

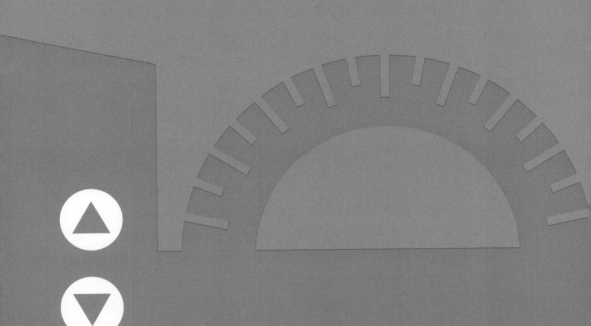

Designing an accessible City

Responding to legislative and regulatory changes on a city-wide scale requires political commitment at the highest levels. This chapter looks at the reaction of one local authority – the City of London Corporation – to the changes in the planning and building regulations. The City of London Corporation is the governing body of the Square Mile, providing local authority services for the benefit of people who live, learn, work and visit the City, the financial centre of London (Figure 2.1). The Corporation's Common Council introduced a comprehensive programme to improve accessibility, prompted by demands from local residents and by staff in the planning and social services departments, who became increasingly aware that disabled residents and workers were being severely constrained by barriers in the built environment.

Figure 2.1 View of the City of London from the south bank of the River Thames: the City's medieval streets, historic churches, listed buildings and modern skyscrapers have, over the last 30 years, gradually become more accessible to London's diverse community.

The inaccessible City

In the 1980s it was very difficult for many disabled people to get around London – no buses, tube stations or black cabs were wheelchair accessible, there were very few dropped kerbs and tactile paving had not been invented, so even crossing the road was difficult. Revolving doors were the only way into most office buildings, ramps at stepped entrances were rare, as were wheelchair-accessible toilets.

It was common to see planning applications for new office buildings with only one wheelchair-accessible toilet – usually located in the ground floor entrance lobby for use by visitors. The perception was that disabled people did not work in the City

so accessible toilets on upper office floors were considered a waste of space – after all, trains, tubes, buses and taxis were not accessible, so a wheelchair user was not going to be able to get into the City. This was, of course, nonsense. There were disabled people working and living in the City in the 1980s – disabled people were and are everywhere – and they needed accessible buildings, streets and public transport. In fact, the social services department occupational therapist was kept very busy with residents who needed adaptations to their homes to enable them to continue living in the Square Mile. As well as residents living in the Barbican Estate, Golden Lane Estate and Middlesex Street Estate, there were also several retired members of the legal profession living in Inner and Middle Temple who could continue to live independently only if their homes were suitably adapted and the shops, streets and services in the City were made accessible. Despite the City's main role as London's financial district, it had and still has a substantial resident population. Today more than 8,000 people live in the Square Mile, more than 400,000 people commute into the City every day for work and more than 10 million tourists visit every year.

Access Adaptations Programme

The Corporation started to change its approach towards disabled people with the introduction, in 1988, of the Access Adaptations Programme (AAP) – with a small annual budget that, over the next 10 years, was used to install dropped kerbs at virtually every road junction in the City, tactile paving at controlled and

Figure 2.2 Platform lift to the medieval Crypt, Guildhall, City of London: following an archaeological dig and the obtaining of listed building consent and planning permission, step-free access was finally provided to the West Crypt in February 2000.

Figure 2.3 Ramp to Wood Street Police Station, City of London: this Grade II* listed building was made accessible to disabled people in 1991 by the installation of a ramp designed to match the existing stone entrance steps.

uncontrolled pedestrian crossings and, where feasible, seats at suitable resting points. Awareness was raised with businesses in the City and improvements were made to access and facilities for disabled people at the Corporation's own buildings. This included wheelchair-accessible toilets for both visitors and staff, induction loops at reception desks and a platform lift to gain wheelchair access to the medieval Crypt in Guildhall (Figure 2.2; a full passenger lift was later installed in the Crypt as part of the major refurbishment to the North Block). Ramps were installed at the entrance of the Guildhall Library and Wood Street Police Station (Figure 2.3).

Improved access to the Great Hall, Guildhall

One of the Corporation's access improvements – the removal in 2011 of three stone steps leading into the Guildhall Great Hall – is worth celebrating, as it demonstrates that an inclusive and now almost imperceptible solution can be achieved in a Grade I listed building. The Great Hall dates from 1411 and sits on top of London's largest surviving medieval crypt. It is used regularly by the City of London Corporation for civic functions, including (since 1502) the annual Lord Mayor's Banquet. With a seating capacity of 900, this vast, cathedral-like space, with a high arched ceiling and 1.5m-thick walls, is also used for many other public and private events.

The west entrance is used regularly as the ceremonial entrance by the Lord Mayor and City Aldermen. It used to have three stone steps leading up from an internal corridor, built as part of a major extension to Guildhall in the 1970s (Figure 2.4). Many different options of how to ramp these three steps were considered.

Initial schemes aimed to retain the existing modern corridor, glass roof and associated stone columns (Figure 2.5). The fire exit from the Guildhall Library (a door opposite the steps) created another obstacle. A good solution could not be found.

Figure 2.4 **Three steps led up to the entrance to the Great Hall, Guildhall, before improvements were undertaken.**

Figure 2.5 The Great Hall corridor, before improvements.

Figure 2.6 **The entrance into the Great Hall is now level.**

However, a major scheme to renovate the Guildhall North Block, and improve Guildhall Main Entrance and the Guildhall Library, provided the opportunity to re-examine the options. This enabled a more extensive intervention in the corridor – the roof and stone supporting columns along the modern corridor were removed and the roof replaced with a new glass structure that allowed unimpeded access across the full width of the corridor. The gentle slope along the corridor is now hardly perceptible (Figures 2.6 and 2.7). It is a very successful solution to what at one stage seemed an insurmountable problem (Figures 2.8 to 2.11).

Figure 2.7 **Today a gentle slope leads to the entrance into the Great Hall**

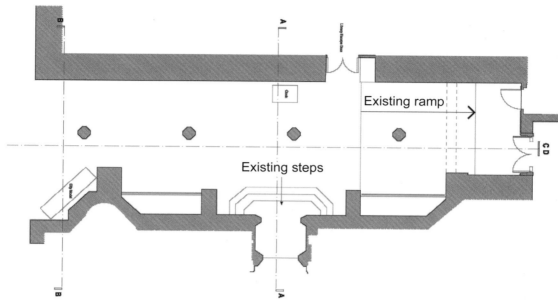

Figure 2.8 Great Hall corridor ground floor plan, before the improvements.

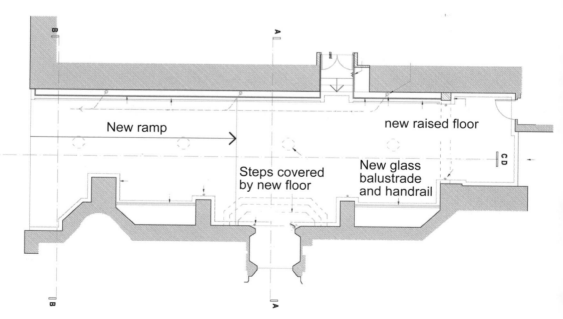

Figure 2.9 Great Hall corridor ground floor plan, improvements as implemented.

Figure 2.10 **Great Hall west elevation, before the improvements.**

Figure 2.11 **Great Hall west elevation, improvements as implemented.**

Improving access to green spaces

Improvements were not confined to buildings within the Square Mile – they were considered at all Corporation-owned buildings, including those in the open spaces managed by the Corporation. Access audits were undertaken of the Corporation's buildings on Hampstead Heath, Epping Forest and Burnham Beeches and the Access Adaptations Programme was used to fund improvements to facilities for disabled people wherever feasible. At Epping Forest the path around Connaught Water was improved to be wheelchair accessible (Figure 2.12), Blue Badge parking bays were designated in the adjacent car park and handrails were installed on the stairs at the Tudor hunting lodge (Figure 2.13). Queen Elizabeth's Hunting Lodge was built in 1543 by order of Henry VIII as a grandstand for royal guests

Figure 2.12 **Easy Access Trail, Connaught Water, Epping Forest: the 1km-long trail has a level, firm, non-slip surface, with benches and passing places for wheelchair users at regular intervals.**

Figure 2.13 **Queen Elizabeth's Hunting Lodge, Epping Forest, was commissioned by Henry VIII in 1543 and renovated in 1589 for Queen Elizabeth I.**

Figure 2.14 **The staircase at Queen Elizabeth's Hunting Lodge, Epping Forest: handrails were installed on the shallow wooden stairs leading to the upper floor as part of the Corporation's Access Adaptations Programme.**

to view the hunt. It was refurbished by Queen Elizabeth I, who reputedly rode her white horse up the stairs! An early and rare example of this type of building, it is listed Grade II* and scheduled as an Ancient Monument, so the design of the handrails had to carefully blend in with the character of the building (Figure 2.14). Today the adjacent visitor centre, The View (Figure 2.15), has a passenger lift to the first floor so wheelchair users and anyone unable to walk up the stairs in the Hunting Lodge can enjoy the view of the forest.

Figure 2.15 **The View Visitor Centre, Epping Forest, 2012 (Freeland Rees Roberts Architects): an oak-framed viewing platform, accessed by a passenger lift and stairs within the new interpretation centre, provides a view of the adjacent Tudor Hunting Lodge and Epping Forest.**

City of London Access Group

Advice from Wandsworth Disablement Association (WDA) was useful when considering priorities for expenditure on the City's Access Adaptations Programme. WDA had advised Wandsworth Borough Council that a small budget earmarked to ramp some steps leading into the town hall would be better spent on installing dropped kerbs to allow disabled residents to reach their local shops and post office – places they wanted to go to regularly as opposed to the very occasional visit to the town hall. (The town hall steps were eventually ramped, once a dropped kerb programme had been established.) The City of London

Access Group – a group of disabled residents and City workers
established by the Corporation early in 1988 – similarly helped
the Corporation make decisions about how to spend the Access
Adaptations budget. The group's members were not passive
recipients of the council's decisions, but actively engaged in the
programme. The group is still very active today.

Dropped kerbs and tactile paving

Making all the streets in the Square Mile accessible to wheelchair
users seemed like a massive task, but the Access Group advised
that the best place to start was where disabled people were most
likely to be. So, the priority was to improve the streets around St
Bartholomew's Hospital and the Bart's Access Action Area was
launched. One of the City's highway engineers, accompanied by
me and members of the Access Group – including wheelchair
users, blind and partially sighted people, elderly people who
used walking sticks and others with personal experience of

Figure 2.16 **A unisex, wheelchair-accessible WC was installed
in West Smithfield, London, above the underground public
toilets as part of the Access Adaptations Programme.**

environmental barriers – walked every street in the vicinity of the hospital and identified every barrier along the route. Members of the Access Group then advised where to locate dropped kerbs, Blue Badge parking bays and seats. One major improvement was the installation of a new wheelchair-accessible toilet facility above the existing underground public toilets in West Smithfield (Figure 2.16).

Once the streets around St Bartholomew's Hospital were made accessible, the group moved on to areas around each of the key railway stations in the Square Mile, so that any disabled person arriving in the City could move beyond the station to their place of work. A Cross City Route from Fleet Street to Aldersgate was tackled next. Eventually, over a period of 10 years or more, the City streets gradually became more and more accessible. This incremental approach took time, but it did result in positive change.

One of the challenges of installing dropped kerbs was highlighted in 1989 by the RNIB (Royal National Institute of Blind People), which wrote to every local authority asking them to stop installing dropped kerbs until a solution had been found that suited blind and partially sighted people as well as wheelchair users. By dropping the kerb, the guide used to alert a blind person to the carriageway was removed, creating the hazardous possibility of walking unawares into a busy road. The government had been undertaking various studies into the suitability of using a tactile surface at pedestrian crossings, and following extensive research at Cranfield Institute of Technology, published guidance on the use of tactile paving at dropped kerbs.[1] The Institution of Highways and Transportation published a useful guide in 1991 incorporating this advice.[2]

Given the historic nature of the City and its many listed buildings, conservation areas and medieval streets, and the use of traditional Yorkstone paving, there was resistance to installing pink- and buff-coloured concrete tactile paving at every controlled (pink) and uncontrolled (buff) crossing. Experiments were undertaken using granite – hand carved to follow the precise specification of the size of the tactile blisters. The AAP funded the installation of granite tactile paving at the controlled pedestrian crossing in St Paul's Churchyard and the Access Group was asked to assess its effectiveness. A compromise solution was eventually agreed – rather than using the very expensive granite tactile paving, the buff-coloured tactile paving would be used on controlled crossings outside historic buildings as it blended in better with the Yorkstone paving. One of the messages – the colour contrast helpful to partially sighted people – was therefore lost, but at least it meant that the tactile message remained and the programme to install dropped kerbs across the City could continue. (The Yorkstone tactile paving on the St Paul's Churchyard crossing has since been replaced by metal studs which, as well as being less easy to see, especially in bright sunlight, do unfortunately create another set of issues, particularly for guide dogs who have been known to catch their paws on the metal studs if the studs start to lift and become uneven.)

Other initiatives, such as the Considerate Contractor Scheme (CCS) and the Considerate Contractor Streetworks Scheme (CCSS), ensured that dropped kerbs, tactile paving and any other street improvements were maintained, and any construction sites or roadworks did not make the route inaccessible. The schemes still operate today and are open to all contractors undertaking building and civil engineering in the City of London. Scheme members agree to follow a code of good practice and are expected to abide by the principles of care, cleanliness, consideration, cooperation, communication and climate. The 'care' part requires the following:

All works will be carried out safely and in such a way that it will not inconvenience pedestrians or other road users. Special care will be taken to make sure that pedestrians with sight, hearing or mobility difficulties are not inconvenienced or endangered and that access is maintained for those in wheelchairs and pushing prams.[3]

Now in its 30th year, the Corporation's CCS and CCSS Award Ceremony presents awards directly to the individual site foreman, giving a sense of pride and commitment on an individual level.

Guidelines for an accessible built environment

A key element of the Corporation's approach to improving access was corporate support for the work. The assistant town clerk monitored progress by holding regular meetings attended by deputy directors of all the key departments, including planning, engineering, libraries, open spaces and social services, and progress was reported annually to the Social Services Committee. This helped to obtain not just a continuing budget to fund the Access Adaptations Programme, but also support for developing and enforcing planning policies aimed at ensuring provision was made for disabled people in all development proposals. Appropriate planning policies were devised and set out in the publication Designing an Accessible City.[4] The guide contained information on statutory and legal obligations, planning policies and practical design guidance indicating how access could be provided. It was very encouraging to walk around the City seeing new buildings designed and built to be accessible because of this work.

Have we now achieved 'an accessible City'?

'Overall, the public realm is much improved: streets particularly, and public transport doing what it can. Developers are far more aware than they used to be, partly because of Access Group comments on planning applications, partly because of the Considerate Contractor Scheme, especially now it includes an Access Award. But some see compliance as a tick-box exercise, and don't think through the practical implications (e.g. refuge points not recessed from the stampeding hordes, or complex routes to accessible toilets).'

Val Southon, Member of the City of London Access Group, 2018[5]

The impact of legislation, regulation, improved technical standards and the political approach taken by the City of London Corporation has seen significant change in the last 30 years. The streets and public realm are now much more accessible and the standard of provision in new office buildings is very different. Half of the City's office floor space has been redeveloped or refurbished since 1990, providing the opportunity to improve the access and facilities for disabled people in the new buildings. Every new office building is now fitted with wheelchair-accessible toilets on every floor (as required by Part M of the building regulations) and level entrances are now the norm across the City (and much preferred to external stepped/ramped entrances). Many listed and historic buildings have also undergone improvements over the years and there are now many examples of sympathetically designed ramps and handrails to the external entrances of listed buildings in the City. For example, the substantial level change at the entrance into St Botolph Without Aldgate was a challenge to make accessible, but the integration of the ramps and steps (without creating tapering steps or unguarded ramps) has

Figure 2.17 **Ramp and steps to St Botolph Without Aldgate, City of London: a series of planted terraces creates an accessible approach to the church. The landing between each flight of steps provides a level area between each section of ramp.**

successfully created a pleasant space to sit as well as making access into the church easier for people attending services, weddings and funerals (Figures 2.17 to 2.19). An added benefit is the ability to host a wider range of concerts and other events in the church as the ramps are now used to wheel heavy sound and other equipment up to the entrance.

Figure 2.18 **Handrails provide support either side of the steps up to St Botolph Without Aldgate.**

Figure 2.19 **The Grade II* listed St Botolph Without Aldgate was made accessible in 2016 by the installation of ramps and the rearrangement of the entrance steps within the enclosed churchyard, while maintaining the visual framing and symmetry of the southern approach to the church.**

Getting to and around London

The 1990s saw change not just in the Square Mile, but across the whole of London, as public transport gradually became more accessible due to initiatives introduced by Transport for London and its predecessor London Regional Transport. By 2000 all black cabs in London were wheelchair accessible, more and more buses were being made accessible and the Jubilee Line extension had opened – the first Underground line with lifts onto all the new platforms and level access onto the trains.

Today all black cabs and all London buses are wheelchair accessible. Over half of London Overground stations and 74 out of a total of 270 London Underground stations are step-free. Transport for London is currently investing a further £200 million to deliver step-free access, so by 2022, more than 100 tube stations will be step-free. This does not seem a high proportion until you consider that the first station opened in 1863, when access for disabled people was not a consideration. The new Crossrail (Elizabeth Line) stations have followed the standards set by the Jubilee Line and will have level access from street to platform and platform to train, making it much easier for everyone to get on and off the trains quickly and safely. Audible announcements are now made on all buses and trains, making it easier for blind people to travel independently. Transport for London is continually improving access to London's public transport facilities and now has comprehensive information on the accessibility of its services on its website[6]. This has made a considerable difference to disabled people commuting into London to work every day, as well as the increasing number of national and international visitors to the city.

Despite improvements, barriers to inclusion persist in the City

Despite this progress, barriers are still being created. A typical example is the building entrance. Although every revolving door now has an adjacent wheelchair-accessible side door (as required by Part M of the building regulations), these side doors are often locked and marked with a sign that says, 'Please use the revolving door', making these entrances inaccessible (Figure 2.20). Automatic sliding doors are encouraged as the best inclusive solution – an entrance that everyone can use rather than one with a separate entrance for disabled people, with bells or intercoms necessary to alert reception. However, most new City office buildings continue to be built with a revolving door and a

Figure 2.20 **A barrier prevents use of this 'accessible door'.**

separate 'special' door for disabled people. Energy efficiency is often used as the reason for continuing to install revolving doors, but solutions such as the curved automatic sliding door can conserve energy and provide an inclusive entrance.

Another issue is the size of some office buildings today, which Sarah Morgan, chair of the City of London Access Group, who uses sticks and crutches to assist with moving about, finds difficult. She commented, 'I'm increasingly conscious of the scale of buildings now, with reception areas and building entrances tending towards vast spaces and therefore significant distances, which test endurance with little opportunity for respite or relief.'

Seating is not always provided in office entrances, and even when it is, it is often very low so not easy to use by everyone. Even where provision for wheelchair users has been made, this does not mean the building is accessible for everyone. Sarah explained:

Going to places becomes a pre-planning minefield involving understanding whether the lifts/stairs/toilets are in the basement or on the level I'm already on, and so on. Worse still is, for me at least, the overwhelming presumption that if somewhere is wheelchair accessible, it's therefore 'fine'. Ramps are tough for people on sticks, not only for the gradients, but also because of the distances they need – a winding ramp is not my preference as it's exhausting and painful. I can't book a 'wheelchair seat' because what is actually meant is a 'wheelchair-sized space of floor to park in', so is no use to a person who doesn't have their own wheelchair.

The City's streets have improved, with better maintenance and management of dropped kerbs and paving and better understanding of how to properly hoard up construction sites. However, the increasing use of footways by construction hoardings can push pedestrians out into the road into single-file protected areas, putting pressure on wheelchair users and stick users to negotiate the narrow space, often with missing or improvised dropped kerbs. Improvements can also be undone. Sarah Morgan is concerned about 'the erosion of pedestrian-only spaces by cyclists freelancing and rushing about'. She reflected:

> Even zebra or pelican pedestrian crossings can be minefields as road users decide they can just move through you, swerving and weaving if they think they have the room, and the advent of headphones plugged into loud music means that pedestrians exist in their own bubble, oblivious to the world around them, so it is rare for me to go out even for a short walk without having to call out to someone to stop them walking into me. It all adds up to an increasingly combative and aggressive streetscape that becomes a battleground. No amount of improved pavement surface can compensate for people being self-centred and arrogant enough to have no consideration for others.

Improved access onto buses and tube trains can also be negated by the behaviour of other travellers. Sarah explained:

Journeys become military-grade strategic plans based around whether or not I might be able to get on the first tube or bus or whether I should allow time for it to be the 4th or 5th that will look sufficiently empty to be confrontation free in terms of getting the right sort of space/seat. Physical infrastructure can make transport less exhausting, but it's usually wiped out by the behaviour of people.

One way forward is to be more 'principled based' and focus on designing for everyone rather than having to modify schemes to be accessible to disabled people. 'The number of new projects and proposals that are still functionally inaccessible without further modification is staggering,' according to Sarah, who views this as an indication that accessibility 'is still seen as something that must be grudgingly incorporated in order to get permission'.[7]

This issue has been highlighted recently by a mobility-scooter user sitting in the wheelchair-designated space on a train being asked to move to make room for a pushchair. This makes for a very challenging time for everyone. A revision of how we design trains and buses to make room to accommodate wheelchair users, mobility-scooter users and children in pushchairs should be the way forward – we want 'an alliance of wheels' not a confrontation!

> It is important that architects and designers work to "design inclusively" – rather than "adapting for disability", which is what happens at present.'
>
> Leicester Disabled People's Access Group (evidence presented to the Women and Equalities Committee Disability and Built Environment Inquiry, October 2016)[8]

Creating an inclusive environment is a continuous process

The City of London Corporation is still listening. Recognising that creating an inclusive environment is a continuous process, the Corporation included in its 2018 draft Transport Strategy a vision of a 'Square Mile that is accessible to all'.[9] Proposals include prioritising the needs of people walking by ensuring pavements and crossings are smooth, level, wide enough to avoid uncomfortable crowding and free of obstacles. Also proposed are new and improved cycle lanes that will make provision for people using mobility scooters, powered wheelchairs and cycles as mobility aids, and developing a new City of London Street Accessibility Standard that sets minimum and desired standards for the design of streets. Detailed access audits will be undertaken of all the City's streets (in conjunction with the City of London Access Group) to assess the current level of accessibility and a Streets Accessibility Action Plan, to be published by 2022, will detail any necessary improvements. Critical improvements will be delivered by 2025, helping to ensure 'an environment where everyone feels welcome and safe and can travel comfortably and confidently'. It is encouraging to know that the Corporation's aim is to make the streets cleaner, quieter and less stressful places, with more opportunities to stop and rest – the aim is to deliver a world-class public realm.

This chapter has illustrated the journey of one local authority, from an inaccessible environment 30 years ago to one considerably more accessible today and yet one where it is recognised that continual reassessment and further improvement is still needed as the buildings, the environment and public expectations change.

Having looked in this chapter at how accessibility is being addressed in the City of London, the next chapter considers one rather special project that aimed to deliver an inclusive environment – the London 2012 Olympic and Paralympic Games. The planning and delivery of the Games illustrates the benefits of going above and beyond minimum regulations and the positive impact that designing inclusively from the outset of a project can have, rather than adapting for disability during the design process or once the building has been completed.

chapter **3**

The most accessible Olympic and Paralympic Games

Going above and beyond the regulations

Much has been written about the success of the London 2012 Olympic and Paralympic Games. Achievements included:

- the approach to sustainability (a total of 2 million tonnes of soil was decontaminated, removing all traces of the polluted industrial past)

- the approach to planting and greening the park landscape to promote biodiversity (the new reed beds, woodlands, grasslands and ponds are now attracting a diversity of wildlife)

- the successful recruitment and training of local people to work on the construction site

- the excellent health and safety record – an accident frequency rate of less than 0.17 (1.7 reportable accidents per one million working hours), significantly better than the industry average

- the approach to diversity and inclusion (integrated across all aspects of the Games)

- the transformation and legacy plans (key to the success of the regeneration of this part of east London today).

However, not very much has been written about the inclusive planning and development process, and the impact that implementing the principles of inclusive design had on the Games and the legacy plans.

For many disabled people, the standard of accessibility achieved at the London 2012 Olympic and Paralympic Games was a unique experience (Figure 3.1). There are many reasons why the Games were considered the 'most accessible Olympic and Paralympic Games in history'.[1] Diversity and inclusion were integrated into the UK's 2005 bid to hold the Games in east London, as part of the promise to deliver 'a Games for Everyone'.[2] For the first time ever, the Olympic and Paralympic Games would be organised by one committee – a major change in how the Games had been organised in the past. This had a huge impact on every aspect of the development and its delivery – from support given by the government and the Mayor of London, to Stephen Duckworth, a disabled business leader and board member of the Olympic Delivery Authority (ODA) being able to champion inclusion at board level, and the

Figure 3.1 **Spectators gather at the Olympic Stadium in 2012.**

London Organising Committee of the Olympic and Paralympic Games (LOCOG) making inclusion in its broadest sense a major element of its work.

As well as featuring in the 'bid book' that helped London win the Games, inclusive design was addressed in the first master plan for the Olympic Park and in the detailed planning applications for each of the venues. The Olympic Delivery Authority, using the Access for All Framework produced by the London Development Agency as its starting point, developed its award-winning Inclusive Design Strategy and Inclusive Design Standards to make sure that the commitments made in the 'bid book' and in the planning permissions were achieved.[3]

Figure 3.2 **The Olympic Park in 2012: gentle slopes provided a choice of routes throughout the park – the result of the ODA's master plan, which aimed to achieve a 1:60 gradient across most of the public concourse.**

The success of the Games was not just because the venue developers met building regulations, or British Standard technical access standards. A coordinated and concerted effort was made to meet best practice. Inclusive access was not just about the provision of ramps, lifts and toilets – as essential as these elements are – but the opportunity was taken to consider accessibility at the very early stages, when the land itself was being remodelled. For example, the aim of achieving a 1:60 gradient along the 3km-long public concourse was addressed at master plan stage and resulted in a choice of accessible routes throughout the park that are still being used today (Figure 3.2).

The integration of access and inclusion

The aim of the London 2012 Games was to provide a Games for everyone, with services and facilities that met all accessibility requirements. To help deliver an accessible 'end to end' experience, a deliberate and coordinated approach from all partners helped to make the Games a success. The aim was to go beyond simple statutory or regulatory requirements in the approach to accessibility and inclusion. Championed at the highest level, access and inclusion formed a key part of the planning and delivery phases, embedded into all employees' thinking and working practices. The Mayor of London set up an Access and Integration Group to help ensure that plans were integrated and to coordinate the high ambitions among delivery partners, including the Government Olympic Executive (GOE), responsible for coordinating and funding the Games, the ODA, responsible for delivering the buildings, the park and physical infrastructure, LOCOG, responsible for putting on the show,

Transport for London (TfL), responsible for ensuring everyone got to and from the Games, and the Greater London Authority (GLA), responsible for preparing London for the Games and the legacy transformation plans. The approach was delivering joined-up accessibility through joined-up planning. Coordinating the planning of the Games and putting accessibility at the centre of all the infrastructure works helped deliver an inclusive environment and left enduring physical and attitudinal changes as a result.

Stratford City Consultative Access Group

The aim of creating a highly accessible Olympic Park and venues by meeting the principles of inclusive design was also one of the ODA's Sustainable Development Objectives, along with 'healthy lifestyle opportunities during the construction of, and in the design of the park and venues, and the involvement, communication, and effective consultation with stakeholders and the diverse communities surrounding the park'.[4]

Planning policy and the use of planning conditions also had a major impact on how inclusive design issues were addressed. An inclusive planning process had, however, started even before London submitted its bid to the International Olympic Committee. Stratford was designated an Opportunity Area in the 2004 London Plan – an area identified as having the potential to provide substantial new jobs and homes. Discussions had been progressing between the developer, Newham Council and the Greater London Authority on a zonal master plan to develop the land to the north of Stratford Underground Station (the land adjacent to what became the Olympic Park and now partly occupied by Westfield Shopping Centre). When the first planning application for the Stratford City zonal master plan was submitted to the Mayor of London's planning team, the inclusive access policies in the London Plan and the Supplementary Planning Guidance Accessible London: Achieving an Inclusive Environment had to be addressed, and an access group was set up to work with the developer on the proposals.[5]

The first meeting of Stratford City Consultative Access Group (SCCAG), held in a meeting room in Stratford's old town hall, was not entirely successful.[6] The group consisted of local disabled people from Action and Rights of Disabled People in Newham – a very active local organisation of disabled people who had been working with the local council and campaigning for better accessibility in the borough for a number of years. The developer had, in good faith, brought a large glass box, inside of which was a model of the site. The aim was to help demonstrate the early thinking behind the scheme. Unfortunately, as the model could not be handled in any way, two partially sighted members of the access group were unable to get a good understanding of the proposal. Peter Lainson, the chair of the group, working with Val Fone, the access officer based at Action and Rights, quickly produced a protocol for the developer's team, setting out some ground rules of how to present to a diverse group of disabled people (see Appendices 1 and 2).

At subsequent meetings, tactile maps were very successfully used to help the two partially sighted members of the group understand the proposals (Figure 3.3). To start with, the tactile maps were very basic but Adrian Cave, the access consultant from David Bonnett Associates, worked hard to improve the usability of the tactile maps.

Figure 3.3 A member of the Stratford City Consultative Access Group uses tactile plans at a meeting in 2007.

The developer, as required by the outline planning permission, was responsible for funding and running SCCAG and appointing an access consultant to advise on the accessibility of the proposals (David Bonnett Associates were employed by the developer throughout the long planning process). The ODA's Learning Legacy website[7] gives a good summary of SCCAG's work which, having started in 2003, continues today on an informal basis, helping to ensure that Westfield Shopping Centre operates and delivers the accessible and inclusive service that SCCAG envisaged (Figure 3.4; see Appendix 3).

When the ODA set up its Built Environment Access Panel (BEAP), SCCAG was used as the model and both groups worked closely together. Having been involved in the initial

Figure 3.4 **Members of the Stratford City Consultative Access Group assess access at Westfield Shopping Centre prior to its opening in July 2011.**

designs for the new homes to be built at Stratford City, SCCAG was consulted on how these homes were to be designed for use by the athletes during the Games (this part of the Stratford City development became the athletes' village in 2012).

The ODA's BEAP transformed into the London Legacy Development Corporation's BEAP after the Games and continues to advise the LLDC today (Figure 3.5). It is made up of members of the original ODA BEAP, members of SCCAG and members of the local diverse community and is involved in and consulted on all key projects in Queen Elizabeth Olympic Park. An example is the tactile and audible map installed at Mandeville Place – the apple orchard and pavilion in the middle of the park designed to celebrate the Paralympic Games. The map (Figure 4.85) was

Figure 3.5 Members of the London Legacy Development Corporation's Built Environment Access Panel assess the draft London Plan in February 2018.

originally to include Braille but after discussion with the BEAP it was designed to be audible and tactile, so accessible to a much wider range of people.

An inclusive planning process

Inclusive design was established as a key objective from the outset of the Olympic, Paralympic and Transformation planning process. This design philosophy was clearly illustrated in the ODA's Design and Access Statement (the access element of which was prepared by BuroHappold's Disability Design Consultancy), submitted with the master plan planning application:

Underpinning all of the design proposals is the aim to create a fully accessible environment. This not only relates to the physical interventions that are planned but also the way in which they will be delivered. Accessibility and inclusion in its widest sense is addressed in terms of employment creation, the aspiration for training, as well as social and economic improvements. This will be realised in the immediate terms of the Games development and the longer term delivery of the legacy transformation, which will act as a platform and framework for the future legacy communities.[8]

This was reinforced by a number of conditions attached to the planning permission granted by the Mayor of London in 2007.[9] The ODA had to submit for approval an Inclusive Access Strategy setting out the arrangements to implement, monitor and review the commitments to inclusive access. A protocol between the ODA and the local planning authority was established to ensure that the principles of inclusive design informed and were integrated into the detailed design of the Olympic development and legacy works. Not only was the ODA required to ensure that the best standards of inclusive design, as opposed to minimum standards, were used to inform and advise design, but the ODA was also required to:

- produce Inclusive Access Standards
- apply the Inclusive Access Strategy and Standards to all projects
- establish a Built Environment Access Panel (BEAP) and an Accessible Transport Panel (ATP), which were to draw on

expert advisors from government, organisations of disabled people and the private sector

- enable the BEAP and ATP to meet regularly to provide technical and strategic advice to the ODA and monitor implementation of the Inclusive Design Strategy and Standards.

This process amply demonstrated compliance with the London Plan inclusive design policies. The fact that this process was a requirement of the Legacy Transformation phases also helped to ensure continuation of this robust inclusive design process by the London Legacy Development Corporation today.

Compliance procedure

A key to the effectiveness of the Inclusive Design Strategy was the ODA's compliance procedure. It is unfortunately common to see a high standard of inclusive access submitted in planning applications, well illustrated in the drawings and articulated in the Design and Access Statement, but to lose many of the accessible elements during the planning negotiation process or in the later detailed design and construction stages. This did happen to an extent at Stratford City, where some of SCCAG's achievements at planning application stage did not see their way through the construction phase – various access audits undertaken post completion at Westfield Shopping Centre and at the athletes' village found some provisions had been omitted. This, on the whole, did not happen at the ODA as the inclusive design advisor had sufficient authority to work with the project teams, advising them on their approach to inclusion, using a regular reporting mechanism based on compliance with the

ODA's Inclusive Design Standards. Design teams, who all received inclusive design and disability equality training, were required to use standardised conformance reports as part of the ongoing design management process, which allowed the ODA to make informed decisions on whether the level of inclusive design provision was acceptable or not.[10] A conformance report had to be completed for all aspects of a design that was covered by the ODA's Inclusive Design Standards, with each applicable building element briefly described along with the reason it did or did not comply with the standards. Where the design failed to meet the standard and did not offer an equivalent level of accessibility, this had to be described and justified. The completed form had to be sent to both the ODA project sponsor (the officer with overall responsibility for that particular building) and the ODA principal access officer, along with drawings showing the proposed design. A report was required if the proposal failed to achieve the standard at all stages of the design process, during and at completion of the particular work stage. The effective implementation of this process was successfully demonstrated by the accessible experience disabled visitors enjoyed during the Games. This process is still used today by the LLDC.

Disabled people played a key role

Disabled people were integral to the design process and key to its success – employed as professional access advisors, access consultants and as representatives of local community organisations and engaged in effective consultation as members of the ODA's Built Environment Access Panel.

A key element to the ODA's, and now the LLDC's, success is the direct involvement of disabled people – there was, in addition to the BEAP, an ODA Community Access Forum which was attended by local disabled people and organisations of disabled people. Disabled people were, however, not just consultees as many of the professional staff employed by the GLA, the ODA and LOCOG were disabled. David Morris (Figure 3.6), the Mayor of London's disability advisor, was hugely influential in shifting attitudes, developing policy and assisting the GLA, the ODA and LOCOG in the development of their approach to diversity and inclusion, before he sadly and very prematurely died in 2010. The ODA's inclusive design advisor and inclusive transport advisor and LOCOG's access advisor all had their own personal experience of disability and impairment, which added to their professional

Figure 3.6 **David Morris, the Mayor of London's disability advisor, working in his flat in London, in 2007.**

expertise. This made a huge difference, not just for their professional colleagues but also to all the consultants working on the project too – it is much harder to dismiss a comment or issue when you can see the impact it will have on the people directly in front of you.

The involvement of disabled people in the park continues today. As well as continuing with the BEAP, the LLDC helped to set up the Global Disability Innovation Hub (GDIH) – another excellent example of the legacy success of the London 2012 Paralympic Games. Launched by the Mayor of London, Sadiq Khan, in 2016, the GDIH was founded by a collaboration between the LLDC, University College London (UCL), London College of Fashion – University of the Arts, Loughborough University, Leonard Cheshire Disability, the Victoria & Albert Museum, Sadler's Wells and the Helen Hamlyn Centre for Design. Based at UCL Here East, Queen Elizabeth Olympic Park, the GDIH works with local communities, academics, experts and disabled people to drive innovation, co-design and creative thinking.[11] The Hub's vision is to make a positive difference to the lives of the one billion disabled people around the world by 2030. Its mission is to change the way we think about disability through co-design, collaboration and innovation. The dedicated research, teaching and practice centre provides a platform for the talents of disabled people and the expertise of practitioners, academics and local communities. Over the next 10 years, the GDIH wants to become the leading place to come to research, study, practise and share disability innovations (see Chapter 6 for details of how the GDIH is improving skills and knowledge).

Welcoming disabled visitors to London

Another aspect that helped to make London 2012 successful was the work the GLA did to welcome disabled visitors to London. Visitors were expected to spend time at other tourist attractions in London as well as going to the Games, so preparatory work was undertaken to ensure that disabled visitors were able to make the most of London's extensive visitor attractions.

One concern was the small number of hotel bedrooms that were accessible to disabled people, along with information available to help disabled visitors find the few hotels that might suit their particular access needs. So the Mayor of London commissioned Live Tourism, a consultancy specialising in accessibility and quality standards, to undertake a study into the accessibility of London as a visitor destination. Their report, Is London Ready to Welcome Disabled Visitors?[12] provided a snapshot of London's accessibility, identified major initiatives underway to improve access, and made recommendations for intervention by the public sector that would help increase accessibility in the run-up to 2012. Research into the views of disabled visitors staying in London was undertaken (582 online interviews were conducted in November and December 2009), along with desk research into plans and policy documents and interviews with more than 40 key stakeholders in the public, private and voluntary sectors. The report also established baselines against which progress could be measured after the Games. It found that major issues for disabled visitors included access to public transport, the lack of clear pedestrian routes and dropped kerbs, as well as signage and wayfinding in the public realm, facilities in shops and restaurants, staff awareness and the lack of reliable, easy-to-find information. Many visitors looked for budget hotels and bed-and-breakfast accommodation, but accessible rooms were few so disabled visitors were often forced to look at mid-range hotels instead. Provision and quality of public toilet facilities was hugely negative.

The Mayor of London responded by setting up an Accessibility for Visitors Programme. The programme included commissioning Inclusive London (a new website that provided information for disabled visitors), Destination London (an online training programme for the hospitality industry to raise the level of disability awareness) and £4 million towards access improvements along the south bank of the River Thames (see Chapter 4). The City Operations Programme was also tasked with integrating the access needs of disabled visitors. As Paralympic advisor in the GLA's London 2012 Unit, I spent a delightful but very busy summer visiting many London boroughs to help ensure that A Summer Like No Other, London's diverse cultural arts and events programme, with exhibitions, street art and performances, was accessible. Event organisers were asked to provide disabled visitors with access to suitable toilet facilities, information about Blue Badge car parking and accessible public transport facilities. British Sign Language (BSL) interpreters were employed to make events accessible for Deaf[13] people and subtitles were used where possible. Vocal Eyes provided audio description so that blind and partially sighted people could enjoy the events and Deaf and disabled artists and performers showcased the best of Liberty – the Mayor of London's annual disability arts festival.

Access audits were undertaken of all the routes to be used for the Discovery Trails around central London (trails illustrating interesting and historic buildings and locations) and boroughs were asked to install dropped kerbs where needed. The Olympic and Paralympic mascots – used as route finders along the trails – were raised on plinths so as not to be an obstacle to pedestrians (Figure 3.7).

Figure 3.7 **Thames Riverside Walk, London, September 2012: Wenlock, the London 2012 Olympic mascot, is raised on a plinth to avoid being a hazard to pedestrians as he guides visitors along one of the Discovery Trails around London.**

The Games were shown on giant screens at four Live Sites – Hyde Park, Victoria Park, Trafalgar Square and Potters Field – so facilities such as accessible viewing platforms, BSL interpretation and subtitles had to be made available. The training given by LOCOG to the huge volunteer force – 70,000 Games Makers – included disability equality training to help ensure that an accessible welcome was given to all visitors. Reasonable adjustments were made to enable disabled people to become volunteers – including use of adapted cars so that disabled volunteers could taxi athletes between their hotel and the venues. Another legacy from the Games is the GLA's Team London Ambassador volunteering programme, with more than 600 volunteers welcoming visitors to London's busiest tourist locations every summer.

After the Games, a conference was held in City Hall – 'An Accessible and Inclusive Games: The London Story' – with presentations from key participants in the GLA's Accessibility for Visitors Programme, the ODA and LOCOG, which summarised the work undertaken to make London 2012 'the most accessible Games ever.'[14] A follow-up study was commissioned in 2013 and the results were published in a report titled Games Changer? An Evaluation of London as an Accessible Visitor Destination.[15] As well as consumer, stakeholder and desk-top research, based on the interviews undertaken in 2009, a series of case studies (written and video) illustrating good practice in delivering an accessible visitor experience were undertaken (see Chapter 4). The report found that London had become a more accessible city across all aspects of the visitor experience since 2009, but there were opportunities to build on those achievements.

The Mayor of London has continued to include policies in the London Plan to promote the provision of more accessible hotel bedrooms, but obtaining accurate information is still difficult. The latest study, undertaken by the GLA in 2017, states:

There is currently no existing data source with information on accessible rooms. However, limited information is available for some hotels via specific online access guides. Establishments themselves tend not to provide information on the number of accessible rooms available nor do they tend to provide comprehensive information on the design of facilities within bedrooms and bathrooms. Consequently, there can be inconsistencies as to what an accessible room is – for some hotels this can mean wheelchair accessible, whereas for others it can refer to rooms that can cater for other disabilities like blindness.[16]

An inclusive development process from the outset

By applying an inclusive development process from the very start of the London 2012 project and by monitoring its implementation throughout the design, planning, construction and in-use stages, the Mayor of London, the Olympic Delivery Authority and the London Organising Committee clearly demonstrated how effective and successful this approach can be.

The concept of an inclusive development process was not new, but London 2012 was the first time it was used effectively at such a large scale. The concept was first developed by the

Access Committee for England and the Centre for Accessible Environments back in the 1990s, included in the government guide Inclusive Projects, published by DPTAC (the Disabled Persons Transport Advisory Committee) in 2003, and articulated in the London Development Agency's Inclusive Design Toolkit in 2007.[17] The concept was further refined by NRAC (the National Register of Access Consultants) for the draft overlay of the RIBA Plan of Works. Included in the Greater London Authority's Accessible London Supplementary Planning Guidance to the 2011 London Plan,[18] the draft Plan of Works overlay helps to illustrate where in the design process inclusive design activity should take place. Advice on integrating inclusive design principles into the development process from the outset has, for the first time, been included in the 2018 edition of British Standard BS 8300.[19]

The LLDC amply demonstrated the benefits of making inclusive design a key part of the procurement and tendering process when a new concept in inclusive living – the multi-generational home – emerged as a direct result of this policy. PRP Architects responded with this new typology when bidding to design new homes at Chobham Manor, a residential development site located just north of what is now East Village (the athletes' village in 2012). Built by Taylor Wimpey, these three-storey, three-bed homes include a self-contained studio annex for use by a grandparent, a returning student or a disabled adult member of the family wanting to live independently (Figures 3.8 to 3.11).

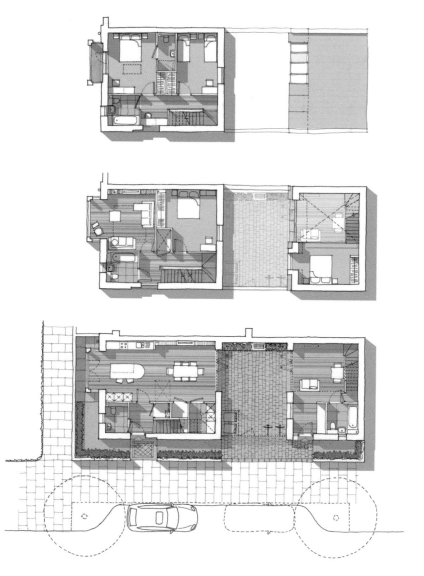

Figure 3.8 **Multi-generational house, Chobham Manor, Queen Elizabeth Olympic Park, London, 2017 (PRP Architects): the floor plan shows the home split into three separate elements – a three-bedroom house, a shared courtyard and a one-bedroom annex with its own living space, kitchenette and bathroom, allowing the occupant independence while being in close proximity to the main house for support if needed.**

Figure 3.9 **Located at the end of the terrace, the multi-generational house results in a typology that successfully turns the street corner.**

Figure 3.10 **Multi-generational house: both the main house and the annex have their own front doors onto the street, with an on-street parking space adjacent.**

Figure 3.11 **A model of the multi-generational house illustrates the relationship of the main house to the annex. The master plan allowed for a variant of the annex to be developed as a single-storey, wheelchair-accessible home.**

The revised British Standard also sets out, in Section 5, guidance on site planning, the position of buildings and their features, navigation, orientation and wayfinding, the legibility of space, and the principles of two senses (audible/tactile and visual). A scheme's final accessibility can be impacted by topography and the location of buildings across the site, and the position of entrances and other features and how they are arranged, so it is important to give early consideration to these factors. This is well illustrated in Queen Elizabeth Olympic Park, where the large number of bridges required (35 during the Games) to cross the canals, rivers, railway lines and roads had a major impact on the layout of the park and the location of the venues. Making inclusive access for disabled people a key part of the strategic policy at an early stage meant that the 3km-long public concourse through the park and the bridges – temporary bridges needed during the Games and those still in use today – were all easily accessible.

Committing to inclusion from the outset also makes it easier for designers to demonstrate how access and inclusion has been addressed in the Design and Access Statement submitted at planning application stage. It brings about a quicker progression at building control stage and allows for a clear monitoring process to highlight shortfalls during construction, making sure any changes are not detrimental to the scheme's accessibility before it is too late. Committing to inclusion from the outset makes sense for the client, the contractors, future building owners and future users.

As well as a more efficient and smooth development process, there is also a clear business case for following the advice in the British Standard and embedding inclusive access from the very start of every project – both large and small.

A visit to Queen Elizabeth Olympic Park today illustrates the lasting impact good inclusive design has had on the success of not just the venues, but the park and landscape too. Access and inclusion was integrated throughout the whole planning, design and construction process and in the management of the facilities in use. The result was a truly accessible experience for everyone.

The next chapter looks at some other examples of good inclusive design but also highlights how the devil is in the detail and attention to the smallest building element is essential if accessibility is to be ensured.

chapter 4

The good, the bad and the inaccessible

Chapter 3 demonstrated what is being achieved in east London, where a holistic approach to inclusive design is integrated into the development process from the outset. This approach is increasingly being implemented in schemes where the client has put people first and embraced and championed inclusive design principles, resulting in a building that really does work for everyone. It is worth celebrating this and looking at how this has been achieved.

This chapter starts with a look at several new and refurbished buildings that have achieved a high standard of inclusive design by addressing the principles from the outset and championing inclusion throughout the project. It was difficult to choose which places to celebrate, so I have included some unusual buildings that originally seemed impossible to make accessible but over the years attitudes, circumstances and determination have produced some great results. A concerted effort to put accessibility and inclusion at the forefront can lead to very positive outcomes.

However, it is always difficult to describe any building as fully accessible, as so many aspects of the design and the management of the building in use can affect the experience of both staff and visitors. So, particular elements of accessibility that work well have been highlighted, along with elements that could have been better.

Unfortunately putting inclusive design principles into the project brief from the outset has not yet become business as usual and there are a lot of places where an inclusive design approach has not been followed, so I follow up the good with the bad. There are, sadly, even iconic and award-winning places where the detail of accessibility has been poorly addressed. So I finish this chapter by looking at some common design pitfalls and some easy things to get right. The devil is so often in the detail. Where good inclusive design is missed, the experience for many people can be disappointment or, at worst, inability to even reach the building or place altogether. We are on a continuing journey and still have a way to go before we achieve an inclusive environment.

The Sill National Landscape Discovery Centre, Northumberland

The Sill visitor centre on Hadrian's Wall, in Northumberland National Park, opened in the summer of 2017 with excellent access and facilities for disabled people – delivered in a way that demonstrates good inclusive design, considered and implemented from the outset of the project (Figures 4.1 and 4.2).

Figure 4.1 **The Sill National Landscape Discovery Centre, Northumberland National Park, 2017 (JDDK Architects): the visitor centre blends into the Northumbrian landscape.**

Figure 4.2 **The Sill Discovery Centre, Northumberland: seats and tables located outside the main entrance provide a good picnic spot on a sunny day.**

Figure 4.3 **The Sill Discovery Centre, Northumberland: the reception desk, lift and stairs to the upper floor are logically located in the spacious entrance foyer.**

Figure 4.4 **The Sill Discovery Centre, Northumberland: the grassland roof is wheelchair accessible, with passing places along the way and a seat to stop, rest and enjoy the view at the top.**

The brief prioritised enhancing and maximising the visitor experience – a building that would attract, excite and inspire people, helping them to make the most of their exploration of the landscape. Making accessibility a definite part of the client's brief from the start has resulted in a building that is open, easy and comfortable to use, with a comprehensive Access Statement on its website describing all the facilities for disabled people.[1]

The Sill National Landscape Discovery Centre comprises:

- a publicly accessible grassland roof
- free permanent exhibition space, where visitors can learn about landscape, culture and heritage
- temporary exhibition, learning and events spaces
- 90-seat café selling local produce
- 86-bed youth hostel with two wheelchair-accessible bedrooms
- shop with local produce, arts and crafts
- rural enterprise hub for new and emerging rural businesses
- tourist information centre
- Changing Places toilet.

The place immediately has a welcoming feel – from the point of arrival, with lots of wide parking bays designated for use by disabled visitors, to the large automatic doors at the front entrance. The reception desk is logically placed and welcoming and there is plenty of seating and space to linger in the entrance foyer (Figure 4.3). A gentle ramp circulates through the ground floor exhibition space, and the wheelchair-accessible WCs and the Changing Places toilet are all clearly marked, as are the clear signs to the lift and stairs and to the upstairs café, which has panoramic views of the adjacent countryside. The needs of all visitors have clearly been well considered.

The centre was named after the adjacent Great Whin Sill – the volcanic crag on which Hadrian's Wall is partly built. The building sits on a restricted site but manages to make the most of this rugged landscape and its unique setting within the Hadrian's Wall UNESCO World Heritage Site. Fantastic views (on a clear day) can be had from the most dramatic and unusual element of the building – the publicly accessible grassland roof (Figures 4.1 and 4.4). A meandering path leads up from the garden, past the café, up and over the roof, giving increasingly good views over Hadrian's Wall and the wonderful Northumberland landscape. Not only does the path (sloped at a gradient of 1:21) provide an exciting route to the top of the building, but it also gives a step-free route from the ground floor to the café on the first floor for anyone who is unable to use the lift or the stairs. The path is the reason the Sill visitor centre should be celebrated and why it is included in this book.

Along the way the grass roof is planted either side of the path with plants that replicate the unique natural grasslands from the surrounding area, providing a way of interpreting the natural landscape. There are level resting places with timber seats along the route. The surface of the path is a permeable slip-resistant plastic grid to help maintain the natural grassland feel. It is manageable for most wheelchair and mobility-scooter users, but some wheelchair users may find it a bit juddery and some stick users may find their stick gets caught in the grid.

Feedback has been very positive – one reviewer on Euan's Guide said:

We were so impressed – it's just opened, and they have a full Changing Places toilet in the visitors area, highly accessible café and ramped access to the roof garden for views along Hadrian Wall. The exhibition area had a lot of displays accessible from wheelchair height and was very interactive. We had a great day out and felt it had been designed very considerately for wheelchair users – even the circular benches outside had been designed with space at each one for a wheelchair to access the table.[2]

Another reviewer on the website commented favourably about the youth hostel at the Sill:

It's such a relief when a place has been built to high standards with wheelchair access in mind. This recently opened hostel has step-free access to all areas, with good-quality bathrooms for its accessible rooms and clean, spacious accessible loo in the dining room area.[3]

The two accessible hostel bedrooms provide a valuable resource. However, these bedrooms are popular family rooms and are not reserved solely for disabled guests, so they may not always be available for wheelchair users. In addition to this, the number of beds (five) in the room may make manoeuvring difficult for those using a large wheelchair.

The Sill project was funded by a £7.8 million Heritage Lottery Fund grant, part of a seven-year investment plan to increase visitor numbers to the Northumberland National Park and Hadrian's Wall World Heritage Sites. From the outset, the client, Northumberland National Park Authority, aimed to transform how people of all ages and all backgrounds experience the wonderful Northumberland landscape. The architect, JDDK Architects, the principal designer, Gardiner and Theobald, and the landscape architect, Glen Kemp, have certainly achieved this (Figures 4.5 to 4.8). The Sill won a RIBA North East Award, was highly commended in the RICS Awards North East and was awarded the 2019 Civic Trust Selwyn Goldsmith Award for Universal Design.[4]

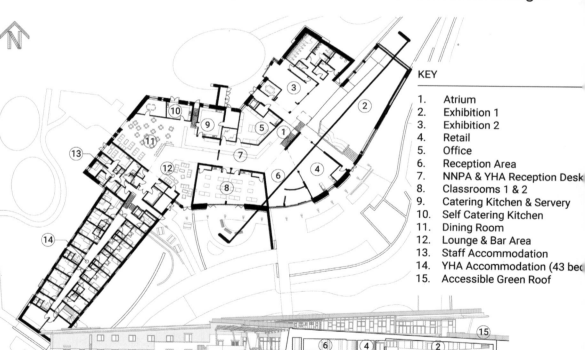

KEY

1. Atrium
2. Exhibition 1
3. Exhibition 2
4. Retail
5. Office
6. Reception Area
7. NNPA & YHA Reception Desk
8. Classrooms 1 & 2
9. Catering Kitchen & Servery
10. Self Catering Kitchen
11. Dining Room
12. Lounge & Bar Area
13. Staff Accommodation
14. YHA Accommodation (43 bed
15. Accessible Green Roof

Figure 4.5 The Sill Discovery Centre, Northumberland: ground floor plan.

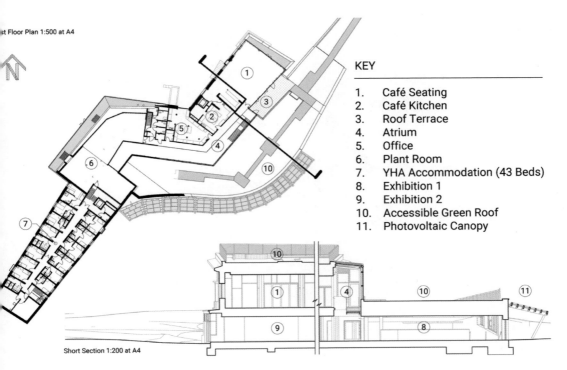

First Floor Plan 1:500 at A4

KEY

1. Café Seating
2. Café Kitchen
3. Roof Terrace
4. Atrium
5. Office
6. Plant Room
7. YHA Accommodation (43 Beds)
8. Exhibition 1
9. Exhibition 2
10. Accessible Green Roof
11. Photovoltaic Canopy

Short Section 1:200 at A4

Figure 4.6 The Sill Discovery Centre, Northumberland: first floor plan.

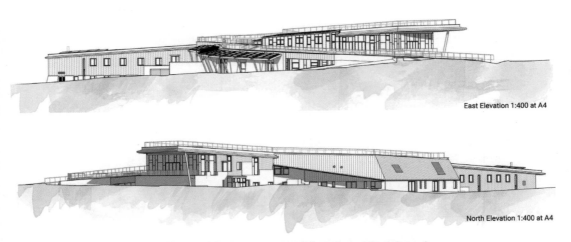

East Elevation 1:400 at A4

North Elevation 1:400 at A4

Figure 4.7 The Sill Discovery Centre, Northumberland: east and north elevation.

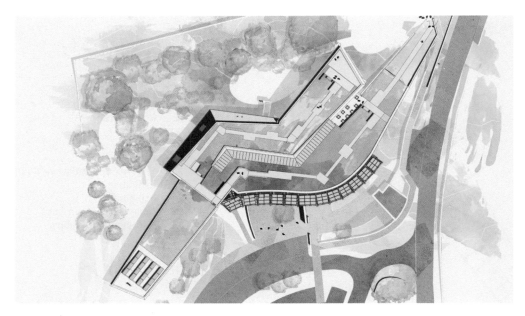

Figure 4.8 **The Sill Discovery Centre, Northumberland: roof plan.**

Portway Lifestyle Centre, Sandwell, West Midlands

The Portway Lifestyle Centre in Sandwell (Figure 4.9) demonstrates how an inclusive approach to the use of a building – the integration of local community health and social care services alongside leisure facilities, all under one roof – can benefit the health and wellbeing of the whole community. Designed by The Design Buro Architects, the £18 million scheme (Figure 4.10) includes a four-court sports hall, hydrotherapy pool, gym and weight area, dance studio, climbing wall, outdoor 3G football pitch, life-trail outdoor exercise area, multipurpose activity room, GP surgery, sensory room and cafeteria[5].

A tactile map (Figure 4.11) at the main entrance explains the simple and legible layout of this single-storey building. A direct route from the main entrance leads to the GP surgery, with a 'rainbow' street providing access from the reception desk to all the leisure facilities (Figure 4.12). The colour of the stained-glass windows in the corridor is echoed in the colour coding of each leisure facility, helping to show the way to the various facilities as well as making the well-lit 'rainbow street' a pleasure to use.

It is a shame that the prominent corner entrance is accessed via a long dog-leg ramp and a flight of stairs, but there is level access from the car park and the parking bays designated for use by disabled visitors at the rear of the building.

Funded by Sport England's Iconic Facilities Fund, which aims to create beacons for grassroots sport, the scheme is designed to promote inclusion, independence and wellbeing and encourage more people to participate in sport. With the emphasis on helping and supporting disabled people, the centre includes the following facilities:

- a tactile map of the building, located in reception
- colour contrast and Braille signs for all key areas of the building
- power-assisted doors located throughout the building
- a Changing Places toilet
- a wayfinding audible-navigation tool to support blind and partially sighted users
- hoist facilities in the changing areas and for access into the hydrotherapy pool
- a virtual signing service on a tablet device
- a dog spending area for guide dogs and other assistance dogs near the 3G football pitch.

Figure 4.9 **Portway Lifestyle Centre, Sandwell, West Midlands, 2013 (The Design Buro): the centre is located on a hill and the corner entrance is accessed via a long dog-leg ramp and a flight of stairs, but there is a level entrance from the rear car park.**

Figure 4.10 **Portway Lifestyle Centre, Sandwell, West Midlands: A prominent canopy and glazed lobby announces the entrance into the building providing a landmark on the high street.**

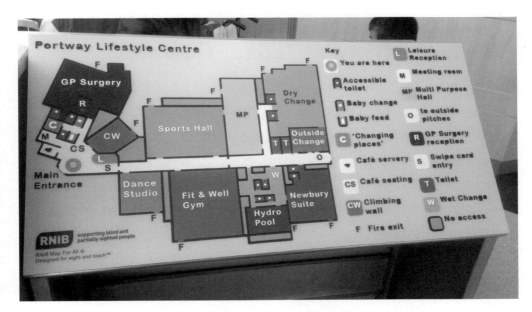

Figure 4.11 **Portway Lifestyle Centre, Sandwell, West Midlands: a tactile map at the entrance assists navigation and orientation.**

Figure 4.12 **Portway Lifestyle Centre, Sandwell, West Midlands: use of colour, glazing and lighting to create a 'rainbow street' further assists wayfinding.**

Frank Barnes School for Deaf Children, King's Cross, London

Dual use has positively impacted on the accessibility and inclusivity of the whole building at the new Frank Barnes School. Co-located with Kings Cross Academy, inclusive design considerations were paramount for both schools from the outset (Figures 4.13 to 4.19). Located on the ground and first floors of the new Plimsoll Building, a 14-storey residential building in the heart the King's Cross development, the two schools share the building, creating a unique learning environment for both Deaf and hearing pupils. ('Deaf' with a capital 'D' refers to people who identify as culturally Deaf and whose first language is British Sign Language.) The Academy pupils are taught British Sign Language (BSL) and Frank Barnes School is bilingual, enabling the children from both schools to communicate, play and learn together. There are sign language classes for staff, carers, parents/guardians and governors to encourage signed communication throughout. Not only is the design very accessible, but the co-location of the two schools has ensured a very inclusive learning space for all.

Design considerations for Deaf users of the building were based on DeafSpace[6] guidelines, a concept developed by the DeafSpace Project (DSP) at Gallaudet University in the United States. Established in 2006, the DSP is an ongoing design and research project led by architect Hansel Bauman in partnership with Gallaudet's Department of ASL (American Sign Language) Deaf Studies.

DeafSpace Concepts[7]

- **Sensory reach**

  Visual and tactile cues such as the movement of shadows and vibrations can be 'read' by Deaf people. Designs can facilitate orientation and wayfinding and spatial awareness 'in 360 degrees'.

- **Space and proximity**

  In order to maintain clear visual communication, individuals stand at a distance where they can see facial expressions and the full dimension of the signer's signing space, so the space between two signers tends to be greater than that of people using spoken conversation. This can impact on the layout of furnishings and spaces.

- **Mobility and proximity**

  While walking together in conversation, signers maintain a wide distance from each other for clear visual communication, and shift their gaze to scan their surroundings for hazards and for maintaining proper direction. The design of circulation and gathering spaces should enable signers to move through space uninterrupted.

- **Light and colour**

  Glare, shadow patterns and backlighting can interrupt visual communication, contribute to eye fatigue, loss of concentration and physical exhaustion. Lighting and elements used to control daylight should be ▶

▶ configured to provide a soft, diffused light. Colour can be used in the interior design of spaces to help contrast skin tone, highlight sign language and facilitate visual wayfinding.

● Acoustics
Sound can be a major distraction, even painful – especially reverberation caused by sound waves reflected by hard building surfaces. Spaces should be designed to reduce reverberation and other sources of background noise.

With extensive consultation and involvement from Deaf pupils, Deaf staff, Deaf governors and Deaf architect/access consultant Chris Harrowell, David Morley Architects put Deaf users at the centre of the design process to create an environment that is inspiring for all, with both schools now demonstrating excellent accessibility and inclusivity.

The two entrances (one for use by pupils at the beginning and end of the day, and one for staff, visitors and those arriving by vehicle) lead into a spacious, light and welcoming environment. A double-height inner street connects the entrances. A void in the upper floor next to the staircase provides a visual link to the lower level, creating a central hub in the building lit by rooflights in the podium garden above.

The staircases are straight and easy rise, to allow signed conversations to continue uninterrupted, and projecting corners in corridors are curved, providing greater awareness of someone approaching in the opposite direction. The landing balustrading was designed so that it appears to be solid when walking along the landing (when viewed parallel); this can help to reduce vertigo. Seen face-on, it allows views through, for spatial awareness and communication (Figure 4.16).

Corridor lengths have been minimised and lifts are glazed to enable users to see out, communicate and be supervised while using the lift. Doors throughout the building have vision panels so that users can see what is happening in the space beyond before opening them. Classrooms are large enough to ensure sufficient circulation space for signed communication and space for wheelchair users, mobility equipment and personal assistants, and are designed to allow flexible arrangements of furniture that enable good eye contact and visibility. There are quiet spaces and a sensory room for pupils who need quiet time. The immediate external environment of the school has relatively high noise levels, so instead of locating classrooms along the street frontage at ground floor level, the classrooms are arranged along the two internal edges of the playground, helping to avoid distraction. Acoustics throughout the school are designed to optimise conditions for hearing-aid and cochlear-implant users. All fire alarms and class changeover bells are combined audible and visual.

Many of the principles and design solutions implemented in the school – particularly those relating to space, natural light, legibility, visibility, acoustics and visual alerts, can be replicated easily in most buildings, increasing the comfort, safety, usability and inclusivity for both Deaf and hearing people.

Figure 4.13 **Frank Barnes School for Deaf Children and King's Cross Academy, King's Cross, London, 2015 (David Morley Architects): the two schools share a main entrance.**

Figure 4.14 **Frank Barnes School for Deaf Children: there is plenty of space to store wheelchairs and buggies under the stairs.**

Figure 4.15 **Frank Barnes School for Deaf Children: the handrail and step nosing design assists all users.**

Figure 4.16 **Frank Barnes School for Deaf Children: the balustrade design creates a visual link through to the staircase.**

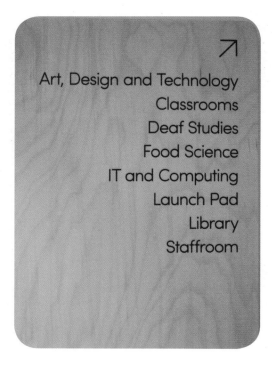

Art, Design and Technology
Classrooms
Deaf Studies
Food Science
IT and Computing
Launch Pad
Library
Staffroom

Figure 4.17 **Frank Barnes School for Deaf Children: the signs throughout the school are clear and easy to read.**

Frank Barnes School for Deaf Children: lobbies at entrances to classrooms are colour coded, aiding orientation and wayfinding.

Frank Barnes School for Deaf Children: the curved walls in the corridors assists visual clarity, providing greater awareness of people approaching.

Royal Liverpool Philharmonic

Attitude is Everything, a charity that works hard to help the live music industry improve access for disabled people to music venues, festivals and outdoor events, has demonstrated what can be achieved when working in partnership with audiences, artists and the industry. The Royal Liverpool Philharmonic was awarded Gold status in Attitude's Charter of Best Practice in June 2018, following the £14.5 million refurbishment and extension of the Grade II* listed Liverpool Philharmonic Hall, designed by Herbert Rowse in 1939.

Caruso St John Architects, the architects of the refurbishment, were awarded the RIBA North West Award 2017 and RIBA National Award 2017 for the 'thoughtful, sensitive and welcome restoration'.[8] The aim from the outset was to maximise access to all parts of the existing and new building for all visitors, performers and members of staff by going beyond the minimum requirements of Part M of the building regulations and so provide a building suitable for increasing numbers of older and disabled patrons. The existing circulation was poorly organised and there was no lift to the upper house, where the best seats were located. Improvements were made to the front-of-house, auditorium and stage areas and the existing rear extension was rebuilt to allow substantial rearrangement of the second performance space and back-of-house areas. A major access improvement was the installation of a new passenger lift in one of the original turrets (Figure 4.20), giving access from the ground floor foyer to the main bar on the first floor. Lift access is now available to all levels of the hall for the first time – the reason this scheme is included here. Step-free wheelchair access is now provided to the upper front of house and the patrons' bar, to the balcony and the best seats, and to the stage from the front of house (access from front of house to the stage prior to the improvements was by exiting the building and re-entering via the back-of-house area). The increased permeability and legibility of the hall has improved wayfinding and orientation, which also supports older members of the audience.

The improvements were undertaken in a way that respected and safeguarded the original listed interior. One of the original design elements of the scheme – the etched musical instruments on the fully glazed entrance doors – demonstrates how manifestation

Figure 4.20 **Liverpool Philharmonic Hall, Liverpool, 2012–2015 (Caruso St John Architects): the new lift is located within the turret on the right.**

Figure 4.21 **Liverpool Philharmonic Hall: the original main entrance doors are clearly highlighted by beautiful etched musical instruments.**

on glazing (ensuring the glass is visible) can be beautiful and functional (Figure 4.21).

Working with the access consultancy David Bonnett Associates, and with an access group established specifically for the scheme, access was also improved to all parts of the auditorium (Figures 4.22 to 4.26), giving wheelchair users a choice of seating locations in the gallery, stalls and boxes. Seats with movable arms were installed, giving wheelchair users the option of transferring from their wheelchair into a conventional seat if they wish to.

A new Changing Places toilet was installed and working practices improved, including:

- relaxed and dementia-friendly concerts, which feature orientation visits, consideration of lighting levels, a British Sign Language interpreter and additional stewards to welcome customers

- an Access Scheme to ensure a smoother booking process for disabled customers (members of the scheme can obtain refunds or credit notes on tickets if they are unable to attend an event due to illness)

- an Access Map and a set of common walking routes, together with a short film which shows visitors what to expect

- a range of programmes and other information provided in large print and Easy Read formats, following guidance from Liverpool Mencap

- an accessible service point in the hall's foyer for the sale of tickets and merchandise

- table service offered to customers if required

- respite spaces for those who need them, available on both the ground floor and upper level

- training for customer-facing staff on how to support blind and partially sighted visitors and people with autism and other neuro-diverse conditions

- annual consultations with disabled customers to enable the venue to continually review and improve customer service, facilities and support.[9]

The new spaces have also enabled more school groups and outreach events to take place. Children can now safely enjoy backstage tours, masterclasses, open rehearsals and events such as 'Baby Voices', 'Toddler Tunes' and 'Little Notes'.

144 Are you an inclusive designer?

On receiving the Gold Award from Attitude, Michael Eakin, chief executive of the Royal Liverpool Philharmonic, said:

 We are proud to have secured Gold status, one of only nine music venues nationally, of which three are in the North, to have achieved this highest standard. Like Attitude is Everything, we believe music is for everyone, and we want to make sure we welcome diverse audiences and artists through our doors to perform, participate in and enjoy music and music-making of the highest quality.

 We are grateful to Attitude is Everything for their support in helping us to better understand Deaf and disabled people's access requirements in our venues at both front and back of house. Their guidance in introducing improvements across our business to improve our welcome and service for these customers has been invaluable, and it is something that we will continue to work on.[10]

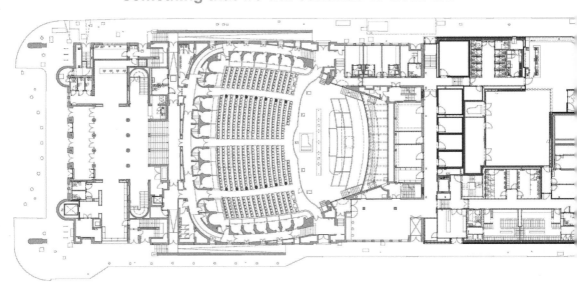

Figure 4.22 **Liverpool Philharmonic Hall: ground floor plan.**

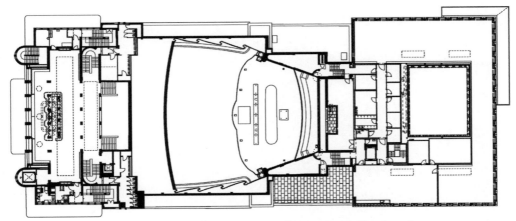

Figure 4.23 **Liverpool Philharmonic Hall: first floor plan.**

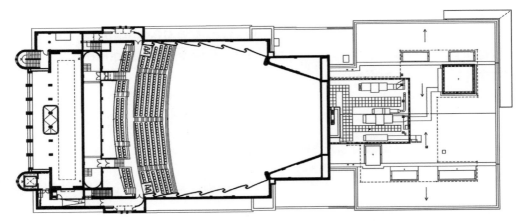

Figure 4.24 **Liverpool Philharmonic Hall: second floor plan.**

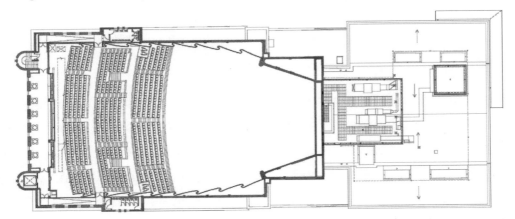

Figure 4.25 **Liverpool Philharmonic Hall: third floor plan.**

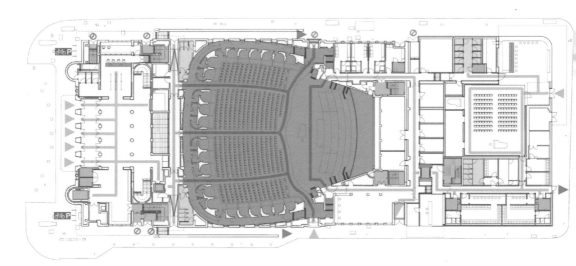

Figure 4.26 Liverpool Philharmonic Hall: the ground floor Access Overlay Plan illustrates the step-free routes now available throughout the building.

Storyhouse, Chester

A redundant 1930s Art Deco cinema in the centre of Chester has been transformed into Storyhouse – a major new city-centre cultural hub including a theatre, cinema, library, restaurant and meeting place (Figure 4.27). The £37 million project has brought theatre and cinema back to the city centre after an absence of over 10 years.

The project director, Graham Lister, worked hard from the outset to integrate inclusive design principles into the development strategy – the reason this scheme is included here – and this shows in the success of the building and the feedback from audiences and users of the community facilities. The project brief included the following requirements:

Where practical all parts of the building will be fully accessible to everyone – and it is important to ensure this is considered throughout the design stage. The design team will consult with local access groups to ensure their views are considered throughout the design process. An independent access consultant will be appointed as part of the design team. The design will use the Arts Council England guidelines for best practice as described in the following publications: Building Inclusion – Physical Access Guidance for the Arts; Disability Access – A Good Practice Guide for the Arts.

Chester Theatre and Library Project Outline Brief, March 2013, Graham Lister, project director

The client, Cheshire West and Chester Council, and the designers, Bennetts Associates, worked closely with the local community, including local disabled people and Chester's Corporate Disability Access Forum, to ensure that the new centre implemented the requirements of the brief and incorporated best practice in accessible design in both public and back-of-house areas. Facilities include:

- spaces for wheelchair users in all three levels in the theatre
- removable seating in the main theatre to enable groups of disabled people to sit next to each other in various parts of the theatre (not just at the front or back)
- a Changing Places toilet in the main foyer area
- seven accessible WCs with a choice of left- and right-hand transfer (with 'left/right-hand transfer' labelled on the door)

Figure 4.27 **Storyhouse, Chester, 2017 (Bennetts Associates): the original 1930s Odeon cinema has been retained and restored and a new rear extension built to accommodate the theatre and a studio.**

This very accessible and inclusive facility has been created while retaining the character and atmosphere of the original 1930s building. Much of the original Art Deco proscenium plasterwork has been retained, creating a dramatic focal point in the building, leading from the foyer into the new theatre beyond (Figures 4.28 and 4.29). A new bright-red steel staircase in the glazed gap between the old and new buildings gives access to the theatre and to the studio theatre above, helping to ease wayfinding and

Figure 4.28 **Storyhouse, Chester: the theatre foyer is used as a performance space.**

Figure 4.29 **Storyhouse, Chester: the original Art Deco proscenium arch above the theatre foyer can be seen from the cinema balcony.**

orientation. The large, very clear directional signs also help the audience to easily find their seats. Not everything is perfect, however. The handrails leading up to the theatre are a moulded, integral part of the balustrade, so are not as visible or as easy to grip as an unobstructed rail. The handrails on the stairs up to the cinema in the original part of the building do not extend beyond the bottom step so do not provide that extra support before ascending or after descending (Figure 4.30).

The library books are dispersed throughout the building, in both quiet areas on the upper floors and in the very public café area on the ground floor – creating an incredibly open and welcoming atmosphere (Figure 4.31). The children's library on the ground floor includes a soft play area for smaller children and is close to baby changing facilities. Above the foyer, which has a variety of seating suiting all needs, hangs a large screen showcasing up-and-coming

Figure 4.30 **Storyhouse, Chester: the original Art Deco staircase leads up to the cinema.**

events, located in the position of the original 1930s cinema screen. Opposite, on the upper floor, is the new cinema, which seems to float above the foyer. The venue also has The Kitchen restaurant and bar and the rooftop Garret Bar (Figures 4.32 and 4.33).

Figure 4.31 Storyhouse, Chester: 700m of library shelving is located throughout the building, with plenty of places to sit and relax nearby.

Figure 4.32 Storyhouse, Chester: The Kitchen restaurant and bar is positioned on the ground floor between library shelves and the relaxed seating area that forms the theatre foyer.

Figure 4.33 Storyhouse, Chester: the rooftop Garret Bar provides a choice of seating, (but the small glass stool is not ideal as it is not very visible).

The main entrance into the theatre foyer is level, with automatic sliding doors. The entrance into the cinema is the original 1930s entrance but has been made more accessible by the rearrangement of the ramp and two entrance steps. However, the stainless-steel corduroy paving at the top and bottom of the steps is not an ideal material – the shiny gloss finish against the white tiled steps does not provide much of a contrast, could be perceived as slippery and its necessary position at the top of the stairs is also close to the top of the ramp so can make turning into the entrance doors more difficult for some wheelchair users.

Storyhouse celebrated disability in September 2018 with a week-long Kaleidoscope Festival. Some 23 local disability-led charities and organisations of disabled people chose events to help celebrate life with a disability and challenge stereotypes. Events were led by disabled people and included a BSL choir, Inclusivity in Dance, Cando Dance Company, a comedy night, Makaton storytelling and rhyme time, talks from disabled people (including 'Believing in yourself', 'Life in pictures' and 'How I found the world when I was young'); and many other talks, films, singing, signing, dancing, knitting, acting, laughing and generally making music to inspire and celebrate diversity and inclusivity. The events team is now assessing the great success of Kaleidoscope and is considering mainstreaming many of the events into Storyhouse's future programme.

The importance of the community agenda – in both the use of the building and the programming of events – was noted by the Civic Trust when the project won the Community Impact and Engagement Special Award in 2018. It is also shown in Storyhouse's tagline: 'This house is your house, what are

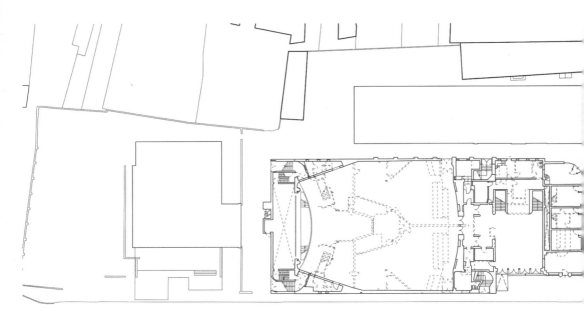

Figure 4.34 Storyhouse, Chester: ground floor plan prior to the redevelopment, showing the extent of the original cinema building.

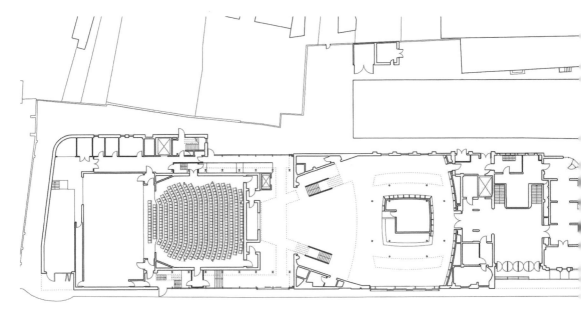

Figure 4.35 Storyhouse, Chester: ground floor plan, showing how the new theatre extension connects to the original building.

you going to do with it?'[11] Performances are captioned, audio described and British Sign Language interpreted, and Relaxed Performances – where sound levels are reduced, lighting levels increased and there is a relaxed attitude to moving in and out of the auditorium – make the performances even more accessible.

A very welcoming venue has been created, enabling a forward-thinking diverse events programme to be part of the usual mainstream film and theatre offerings. Chester now has a fantastic cultural resource in the centre of the city, well used by the whole community, made possible by the sensitive refurbishment of the original building. The scheme retains enough of the original cinema to keep old memories alive, while providing a new extension with modern facilities.

'There is rarely space for wheelchairs in coffee shops and even if there is, simple accessibility through the main doors can be a problem. At Storyhouse there is ramped access leading to a wide-open foyer and from that point onwards you won't find any issue with rolling wherever your mind takes you! There are well-situated lifts to reach the upper floor and both the cinema and theatre are fully accessible, with wheelchair and carer spaces allocated at every performance. Even more importantly for us, there are not only roomy disabled toilets but an actual, fully equipped Changing Places toilet. An absolute rarity, believe me.'

Reviewer on Euan's Guide[12]

HOME, Manchester

In a similar way to Storyhouse in Chester, HOME in Manchester has provided a brand-new cultural centre in the heart of the city (Figures 4.36 to 4.38). The £25 million scheme, designed by Mecanoo Architects, is home to five cinemas, two theatres, flexible gallery space, a large restaurant (Figure 4.39) and bars on each floor. The level entrance, with wide automatic sliding doors, leads into a spacious foyer (Figure 4.40). The obvious sign above the box office announces its presence very clearly and is logically located opposite the entrance doors. The desk height on both sides of the box office counter ensures easy access for both staff and visitors.

Figure 4.36 **HOME, Manchester, 2015 (Mecanoo Architects): the venue fronts onto a public square which is defined by a long continuous bench – the square is not as accessible as it could have been if a greater choice of seating and routes into it had been provided.**

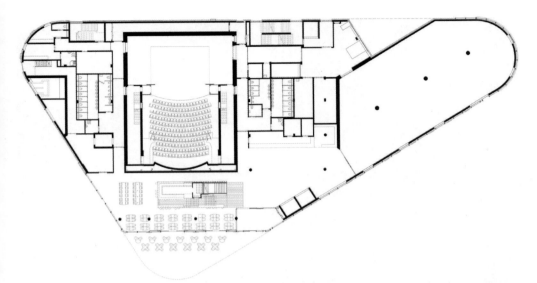

Figure 4.37 **HOME, Manchester: the ground floor plan shows the central location of the stairs, designed to encourage visitors to use the stairs instead of the lifts (this can work against those who have no choice but to cross a crowded area to reach the lifts).**

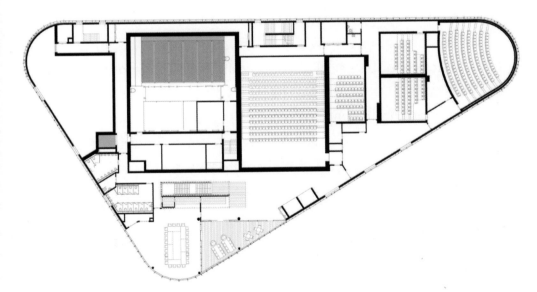

Figure 4.38 **HOME, Manchester: the second floor plan shows the location of the five cinema screens.**

Figure 4.39 **HOME, Manchester: the restaurant has space for buggies and a choice of seating (with or without armrests).**

The wide staircase visually connects the cafes, bars, social and performance spaces on all three levels, helping with wayfinding and orientation. One of the aims of its central location is to encourage visitors to use the stairs instead of the lifts, but this does not always make it easy for people who have to use the lift if, when the centre is busy, they must cross a crowded area to reach the lifts on the opposite side of the foyer (good inclusive design would co-locate lifts and stairs).

The unisex, wheelchair-accessible toilet on the ground floor is conveniently located behind the box office, near to the separate baby-change room and other toilets. It is a shame, however, that the management feel the need to keep the accessible toilet

Figure 4.40 HOME, Manchester: the box office, with its low counter and clear sign, is immediately visible on entering the large, spacious foyer.

locked to reduce the likelihood of vandalism. The RADAR key (used to unlock the WC) is available from the box office, which, although very close, could require a wait at busy times.

The wide staircase (Figure 4.41), with easy-to-grip handrails and the edge of each step clearly highlighted, visually connects the theatre, cinema and gallery with the cafés, bars and social spaces on all three levels, helping with wayfinding and orientation. One of the aims of its central location is to encourage visitors to use the stairs instead of the lifts. The lifts are on the opposite side of the foyer so not far, but when the centre is very busy this may be a bit tricky for people who have to use the lift. The building is located on an awkward triangular site bounded by a railway line on one side and a public square on the other. Reaching the front door from the adjacent streets is a bit of a walk, with one of the pedestrian routes lit at night

Figure 4.41 **HOME, Manchester: the centrally located stairs have easy-to-grip handrails and contrasting step nosings.**

only by borrowed light from the adjacent building. However, the First Street multistorey car park (with Blue Badge parking bays) is opposite and the adjacent public square does provide a focal point and seating area in front of the main entrance, with HOME's café able to spill out onto the square. It is a shame that the public seating in the square is one long bench (without arms), which will not suit everyone.

HOME publishes an access brochure with information on how to book wheelchair spaces in the theatres and cinemas, reservations for assistance dogs, personal assistance and concessionary tickets, and details of selected events with audio description, captioned subtitles, British Sign Language and relaxed performances, along with dates of BSL-led gallery tours and touch tours for blind and partially sighted people.[13]

Manchester City Council's Access Review Forum was consulted and reviewed the scheme several times during the planning and post-occupancy stages, resulting in the project winning the Civic Trust Selwyn Goldsmith Universal Design Award in 2017.

St Paul's Cathedral, City of London

St Paul's Cathedral is one of London's most iconic and well-loved buildings, nationally and internationally. It was designed and built by Sir Christopher Wren after the Great Fire of London in 1666. Improving accessibility at this huge Grade I listed building has not been easy and the subject deserves a lot more space than I have available here.

The cathedral has been considering how best to improve access for a number of years – discussions about ramps first began in the 1970s but change only really started to happen in the 1990s. I clearly remember the excitement of seeing two substantial temporary ramps erected at the cathedral's main west entrance when John Grooms Housing Association held its 125-year anniversary service in the cathedral in 1991. The 24m-long ramps extended way beyond the steps but enabled more than 140 wheelchair users to participate in the service. Dismantled after the event, this focused attention on how disabled people could participate in the daily life of the cathedral.

In 1991, a small lift, originally designed as a fire lift and located just inside a secondary entrance in the corner of the South Churchyard, was the only permanent 'accessible' way into the cathedral. However, the route from the street through the

Figure 4.42 St Paul's Cathedral, City of London: a gentle slope from the gate into the South Churchyard leads up to the accessible (lift) entrance into the cathedral.

churchyard to the entrance door involved three steps and the small call bell to ring for attention was not obvious. The Corporation of London was responsible for the South Churchyard garden and a scheme to replace the railings and redesign the garden gave the opportunity to consider how to provide step-free access into the cathedral. In 1992, the churchyard was repaved and re-laid in a design that sets out the original medieval cloister, forming a pleasant garden and setting for the cathedral. The three steps from the street to the entrance door were replaced by a gentle ramp and a clear sign was erected, making it much easier to find the 'accessible' entrance (Figures 4.42 and 4.43).

An Accessibility Audit Report by John Penton in 2001 helped to further focus attention on what was immediately practicable and what would need careful, long-term planning.[14] The small passenger lift was replaced by a larger, more accessible lift in 2005. While the lift was out of action, a temporary scaffolding

Figure 4.43 **St Paul's Cathedral, City of London: the entrance where the lift is located is very discreetly positioned in a corner of the building at the rear of the South Churchyard.**

and wooden ramp was installed at the north entrance to maintain access for visitors who could not manage the main west entrance steps. This temporary arrangement was a major contributor in helping to progress consideration of installing a permanent ramp at the north entrance – the numbers of disabled visitors able to enter the cathedral was so much greater than when the lift was the only step-free entrance. Use of the lift still required a wait outside and a delay if there were several people wanting to enter the cathedral; in contrast, the temporary ramp demonstrated how useful a ramp was, particularly when events attended by large numbers of wheelchair users were held in the cathedral.

Another temporary ramp was needed in 2008 for a thanksgiving service for Leonard Cheshire Disability to celebrate the charity's 60th anniversary. To provide access into the cathedral for the 170 wheelchair users attending the service, a very long temporary ramp was installed at the entrance to the North Transept – a slightly less intrusive solution than the straight, very long but steep ramp installed at the west entrance in 1991. This helped to further accelerate the debate on how to create permanent step-free access for the large numbers of disabled and older people wishing to attend services and events or to visit as tourists. This event also concentrated minds on the equally important issue of safe egress.

In 2010 another temporary ramp was constructed at the North Transept entrance. This substantial wooden ramp was now a prototype for a permanent installation and stayed in place until 2016, when it was replaced with a metal-framed dog-leg ramp – the ramp still in place at the time of writing (Figures 4.44 and 4.45). This temporary ramp further helped to prove how essential a ramp is and how well it works in this location – particularly well demonstrated in 2012 when it was used for a special service held to celebrate the London 2012 Paralympic Games.

Figure 4.44 **St Paul's Cathedral, City of London: a temporary metal ramp provides access (at the time of writing) to the North Transept entrance.**

Figure 4.45 **St Paul's Cathedral, City of London: the temporary metal ramp to the North Transept entrance was installed in 2016.**

Conscious of the 2010 Equality Act's emphasis on continual improvement, a further review, entitled 'Accessibility for the New Millennium', was undertaken in 2014 by Martin McConaghy, of IDACS (UK), the cathedral's newly appointed accessibility consultant. While recognising the improvements that had already taken place, including refurbished accessible toilet facilities, ramped access in various parts of the cathedral and improved handrails, it was also noted that a main recommendation from 2001 – a permanent ramp at the north entrance – was still unfulfilled.

Another major step in opening up the cathedral has now been made – planning permission was granted in November 2017 for a new permanent stone ramp and new steps to the North Transept entrance, as part of the cathedral's current Equal Access Project (Figures 4.46 and 4.47). The design, by Caroe Architecture, was reviewed and developed with the help of IDACS (UK) Ltd and by an extensive consultation programme with the City of London Access Group and the City of London Corporation's Access Team. The Design and Access Statement submitted with the planning application provides a very detailed explanation of how the proposed design was reached.[15]

The design replaces the current single temporary ramp with a pair of symmetrical stone ramps of six flights each, located either side of a new central stone staircase. Each flight is separated by a landing used as a turning point. To maintain a circular appearance in keeping with the transept entrance portico, a sinusoidal design has been adopted and thus each flight is a slightly different length. The existing stone steps will be retained and covered by the new staircase, which will have more gentle

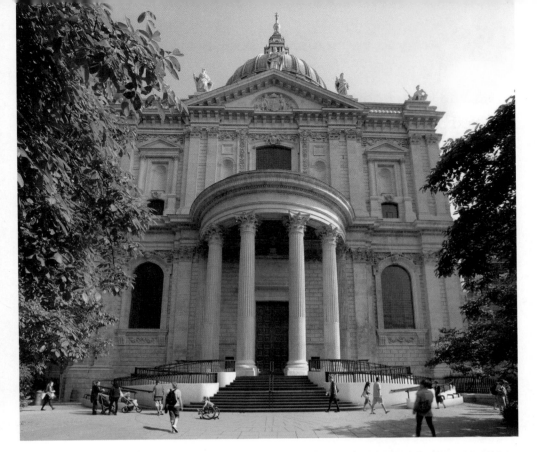

Figure 4.46 St Paul's Cathedral, City of London: North Transept entrance with proposed new ramp and steps. (Caroe Architecture)

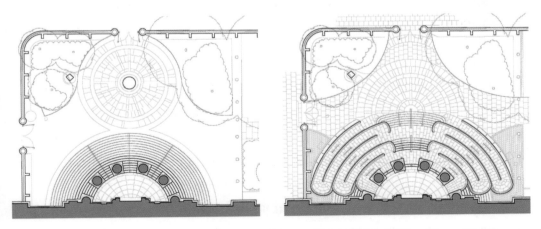

Figure 4.47 St Paul's Cathedral, City of London: this plan (Caroe Architecture) shows the existing staircase and the proposed new permanent ramps to be installed at the North Transept entrance.

risers and longer goings, making the stairs easier for many disabled and older people to use. Although the new ramps will be long and circuitous, rising over 2m, their symmetrical design either side of the new easy-going staircase will provide the best possible solution to what was originally seen as an insurmountable problem, giving permanent and elegant step-free access from the North Churchyard to the North Transept of the cathedral for the first time.

The North Transept is one of three main entrances into the cathedral and has a high communal value as a key connection between the cathedral, the North Churchyard and the wider community. The North Churchyard, a large area of green open space, is well used as a place of rest and respite in a busy part of London, and the inclusion of a ramp at the north entrance is seen as a way of extending the links out to the community, as well as allowing for equal access directly into the cathedral from a main entrance, rather than through a secondary door, as is currently the case.

The approach to the current development has been to achieve the vision of equality for all, not simply an accessible cathedral, and to aim for the highest standards of inclusive design possible within the constraints of such a historic and significant building. It is more than 40 years since installing a permanent ramp was first considered, and providing installation goes ahead as planned, this major achievement will demonstrate that even in the most sensitive locations, inclusive access for disabled people can be accomplished.

National Army Museum, Chelsea, London

The new level entrance at the National Army Museum in Chelsea stands in complete contrast to the substantial (but very much needed) ramp at St Paul's Cathedral. Designed in Brutalist style by Sir William Holford and Partners in the 1960s, the National Army Museum building opened to the public in November 1971. In need of refurbishment, it was closed for three years between 2014 and 2017 while it underwent a huge £23 million Heritage Lottery funded rebuilding programme. The project, by Building Design Partnership, included a major rearrangement of the levels and rationalisation of floor plates – the original 1970s building had numerous split levels and was difficult to navigate. Circulation is now intuitive – the large entrance foyer, along with the new atrium space, visually and physically links all floors and

Figure 4.48 **National Army Museum, Chelsea, London, 2017 (Building Design Partnership): the refurbishment has created a building with a stronger identity within the streetscape.**

Figure 4.49 **National Army Museum, Chelsea, London: the new level entrance with automatic doors is clearly visible from the street.**

Figure 4.50 **National Army Museum, Chelsea, London: a choice of seating is provided in the public garden in front of the building, beside the bus stop.**

opens up views into and out of the museum, creating a more legible, friendly and accessible museum (Figures 4.48 to 4.55).

An extension to the front of the building, removing the original 30m setback, has created a new level entrance fronting Royal Hospital Road. Rearrangement of the public realm, which has a choice of seating and is next to the bus stop, has positively connected the building with the street, making access into the museum easy for everyone.

Figure 4.51 **National Army Museum, Chelsea, London: the original front elevation shows the lack of connection to the adjacent street.**

Figure 4.52 National Army Museum, Chelsea, London: the large and well-lit atrium visually and physically links all the floors, with the reception desk and toilets logically located opposite the entrance.

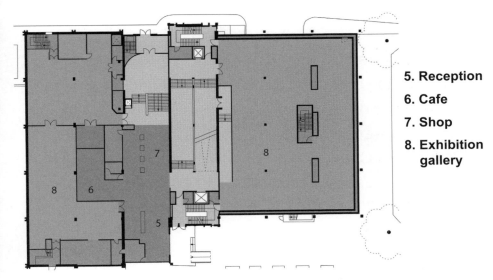

5. Reception
6. Cafe
7. Shop
8. Exhibition gallery

Figure 4.53 National Army Museum, Chelsea, London: the original ground floor plan shows the location of the ramped and stepped entrance, set back from the street, and a building with numerous level changes which were difficult to navigate.

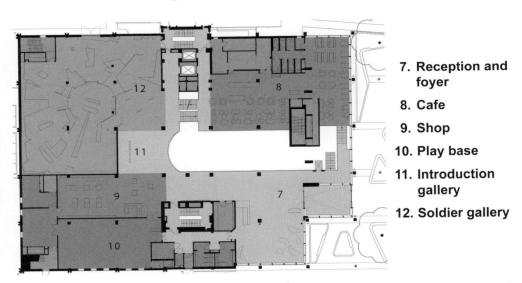

7. Reception and foyer
8. Cafe
9. Shop
10. Play base
11. Introduction gallery
12. Soldier gallery

Figure 4.54 National Army Museum, Chelsea, London: the ground floor plan of the refurbished building shows how the entrance and floor levels have been reorganised to create a much more legible building, so finding your way around is much easier.

The building is now easy to enter, and the location of the lifts and stairs make the museum's interactive displays and exhibition galleries easy to find. Thanks to the improved building access, the provision of café and toilet facilities, British Sign Language tours, sensitive acoustic treatment, ample seating, induction loops, a Changing Places toilet and comprehensive information about access and facilities for disabled people, the museum won the 2018 Civic Trust Selwyn Goldsmith Universal Design Award.[16]

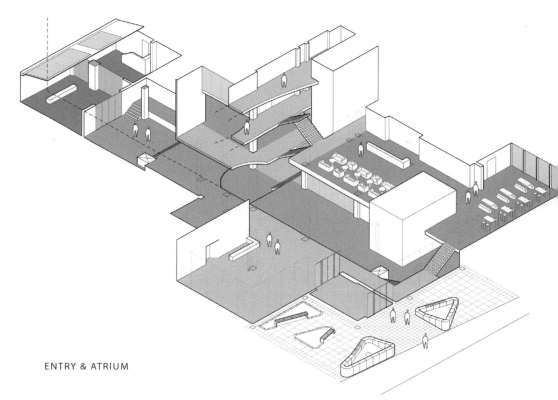

ENTRY & ATRIUM

Figure 4.55 **National Army Museum, Chelsea, London: the entry and atrium axonometric plan shows how the co-location of the stairs and lifts, visible from the large atrium, helps to make all the galleries easily accessible.**

Temple of Mithras, City of London

The relocation of the Temple of Mithras to a new exhibition space demonstrates that even Roman remains can be made easily accessible. Before the relocation, the remains of the Temple of Mithras were reached via a flight of external stone steps from the street, so were not easily accessible. Although the remains were not very substantial, they were all that was left of a temple built in AD 240 dedicated to the Roman god Mithras, so formed an important and exciting sight. The remains had in fact been discovered in 1954 in the ruins of a World War II bomb site. In 1962 they were reconstructed as part of a new office development and relocated in front of the new building's main entrance (up a flight of steps) on Queen Victoria Street.

The solution to the accessibility issue was solved when the 1960s office building was purchased by Bloomberg in 2010, along with all the other buildings in that street block, and a new office development was proposed to house Bloomberg's European headquarters. As part of the redevelopment, the temple was dismantled and relocated near to its original Roman location – street level in the Roman period was seven metres below current street level – and incorporated into a new exhibition space called London Mithraeum: Bloomberg SPACE (Figure 4.56).

The London Mithraeum opened to the public in November 2017. It has a level entrance off Walbrook, and a lift and staircase provide access down to the mezzanine and lower levels of the museum. The ground level has a contemporary and changing cultural exhibition and a display of more than 600 of the 12,000-

plus objects excavated on the site. These objects are described on the available iPads and a dedicated website. The mezzanine level has interactive displays about the Mithraeum, the god Mithras and the religion. The temple is displayed at the lower level and is an immersive experience with light and sound.

Folding seats are available for people who need to rest occasionally, large-print materials, along with torches and magnifying glasses, are available (some areas have very low light so may not suit everyone) and printed information accompanies audio displays.[17] The temple is now step free, well interpreted and considerably more accessible than previously.

Figure 4.56 **London Mithraeum: Bloomberg SPACE, 2017 (Foster + Partners): the Temple of Mithras has now been reconstructed below ground and is open to the public.**

The Bank of England Museum, City of London

The Bank of England Museum, where visitors can enjoy looking at displays of gold bullion and learn about the history of the Bank of England, has its entrance in Bartholomew Lane. When the museum opened to the public in 1988, with an entrance up three external steps, it appeared to be inaccessible to disabled visitors – a good example of the accessibility challenges in the City, which is full of listed and historic buildings. Efforts were made to make the museum accessible – a bell was located at street level for wheelchair users to ask for assistance and handrails were installed on the three entrance steps (Figure 4.57). The handrail is flat as opposed to the rounded and easier-to-grip recommended profile, so is a compromise but one that does work in such a sensitive location. The handrail did not, of course, help wheelchair users who, once a member of staff had been alerted to their presence, were escorted by security staff via the trade entrance in Lothbury, up an internal lift and through the private part of the bank into the museum.

Today this rather tortuous route for wheelchair users has been improved by the installation in 2016 of a Sesame Access Lift in Threadneedle Street. Platform lifts are not an ideal solution as they can break down, can be cumbersome to use and are viewed as being available for wheelchair users only, rather than for everyone. The Sesame Access Lift seems even more of a 'specially for the disabled' solution than the standard platform lift, as it is concealed beneath the stairs so takes time for staff to operate and the unusual sight of stairs retracting and a lift magically appearing from below can make the user into a

Figure 4.57 **Bank of England Museum, Bartholomew Lane, City of London: handrails provide support on the entrance steps.**

Figure 4.58 **Bank of England, Threadneedle Street Entrance: the platform lift is concealed beneath the stairs.**

spectacle, especially in such a busy City of London location. To overcome a short rise in level, a ramp that everyone can use is always preferred to mechanical means.

However, Threadneedle Street is the bank's public entrance (it is used by the public to reach the bank's cashier's desk just inside the entrance) and is located on a very busy but narrow pavement where ramped access would be difficult to install. There was also a desire to retain the integrity of the original Soane façade and columns of the Grade I listed bank (much of Sir John Soane's outer wall, built in 1788, was retained when the bank was rebuilt in the 1930s). The Sesame Access Lift enabled the original Yorkstone steps to be retained while providing a more direct level route into the museum for visitors, a much quicker route compared to the rather tortuous route via Lothbury and the loading bay. It also provides a second step-free route for staff so, despite the time it takes for security staff to operate the lift, the installation of the Sesame Access Lift is a sensible solution in this particular situation. Handrails have also been installed on the steps leading to the cashier's entrance (Figure 4.58). Slightly different to the earlier handrails installed at the museum entrance, the design was based on handrails already used within the bank, originally conceived by Sir Herbert Baker as part of the development of the bank in the 1920s and 1930s.

Thames Riverside Walk at Blackfriars Bridge, City of London

One of the planning challenges during the 1990s was making the Thames Riverside Walk open and accessible to the public along its full length within the City boundaries, from Victoria Embankment to the Tower of London. The deputy director of planning chaired the Riverside Working Party, whose remit included helping to ensure that the needs of disabled people were considered in any proposals to improve public access. One of the big challenges was Blackfriars Bridge. The only access from Paul's Walk – the riverside walk to the east of the bridge – to Victoria Embankment (to the west of the bridge) was a long flight of steps or a very tortuous ramped route that led rather disconcertingly up towards and then through the undercroft of the 1960s British Telecom office building and down another ramp to Queen Victoria Street. This also required negotiating the very

Figure 4.59 **Thames Riverside Walk: the pedestrian route along the Thames Riverside Walk went under Blackfriars Bridge prior to the current Thames Tideway construction works.**

Figure 4.60 **Thames Riverside Walk: a ramp and steps provided access under Blackfriars Bridge prior to the current construction works.**

busy road junction opposite Blackfriars Station to get back to the riverside walk. Consideration was given to building a ramp that cantilevered over the river to avoid such a long detour, but this was far too expensive and difficult to do.

However, in 1998 London Regional Transport investigated further options when plans for a new pier at Blackfriars Bridge were being developed. Listed building consent was granted in 2003 (the Embankment wall is a listed structure) to provide a Yorkstone ramp, with a gradient of 1 in 30, to connect Paul's Walk with Victoria Embankment. Everyone could now continue along the riverside walk – which forms part of the Thames Path – towards Victoria Embankment without any deviation. This was a fantastic achievement, giving users of the new Blackfriars Millennium Pier and its many riverboat services direct access onto the riverside walk from Victoria Embankment (Figures 4.59 to 4.61). This is not the end of the story, however, as pedestrian access along this stretch of the River Thames will soon be even better.

At the time of writing, this route was a major construction site for the Thames Tideway Tunnel (a major new sewerage system being built under the Thames), so closed to the public, and the pier has been relocated to the east of Blackfriars Bridge. Rather than revert to the original stepped route, the City of London Corporation secured the construction of a passenger lift

Figure 4.61 **Thames Riverside Walk: a ramp led down from Victoria Embankment to the route under Blackfriars Bridge prior to the current construction works.**

Figure 4.62 **Thames Riverside Walk: today a passenger lift and stairs provide access from Blackfriars Bridge down to the Riverside Walk and to Blackfriars Pier.**

Figure 4.63 **Thames Riverside Walk: the new circular lift at Blackfriars Bridge is a 'through car' so wheelchair users and mobility-scooter users do not have to reverse out of the lift.**

adjacent to the stairs on the east side of the bridge, giving step-free access to the riverside walk and the relocated pier (Figures 4.62 and 4.63). This new circular 13-person lift is a 'through car', reducing the need for wheelchair users or people with prams or using a mobility scooter to reverse out of it. For the duration of the construction works, step-free access from the riverside walk to Blackfriars Bridge and Blackfriars Station will be retained.

Once the construction works are completed, an accessible route from Paul's Walk, under the bridge and through to Victoria Embankment will be reinstated, along with a new public square to be created over the Thames Tideway Tunnel Foreshore structure. One of the design objectives is to create a world-class area of public realm where people can sit, relax and enjoy views over the Thames (Figures 4.64 and 4.65). Proposals are currently being discussed with the aim of resolving the level differences and creating a simple, clearly defined route from the Embankment under the bridge to Paul's Walk and the pier. Opportunities for appropriate commercial activity to support the new park are also being considered. The circular lift up to Blackfriars Bridge and Blackfriars Station will be retained and a new level route along this section of the Thames Path will be created for the first time – a huge improvement compared to 20 years ago.

Figure 4.64 **Thames Riverside Walk: when the Tideway Tunnel Foreshore structure at Blackfriars Bridge is completed, a new area of public realm will be created.**

Figure 4.65 **Thames Riverside Walk: the completion of the Tideway Tunnel Foreshore structure will resolve the level differences along this section of the walk and create a simple, clearly defined route, as well as a space to sit, relax and enjoy the views of the river.**

Up at the O2, Greenwich, London

From its inauspicious start as the venue for the Millennium Exhibition in 2000, the Millennium Dome has transformed itself into the O2 Arena. With a worldwide reputation, it is now one of the most successful major concert venues in the country. It may initially seem an easy building to make accessible – after all, it has a huge level entrance with a very wide concourse running around the perimeter of the building. It has generous car parking and is close to the Jubilee Line tube station at North Greenwich, which has step-free access from street to train. However, there are multiple venues within the building – not just the main concert arena that seats more than 20,000 people, but the smaller Indigo venue, a multiplex cinema, exhibition space and many restaurants and pubs, which should all provide good inclusive access.

Following advice from David Morris, the Mayor of London's disability policy advisor, a dedicated All Access Advisory Forum (the Triple A Forum) was set up in 2008 and the management team employed at the O2 at that time embraced the ambition to provide excellent inclusive access. With the management team's open and keen attitude to engage effectively with the forum, facilities for disabled people gradually improved over the years. This relationship was clearly articulated in a video made in 2013 for the Mayor of London, as part of a report on London as an accessible visitor destination.[18] The success of the Triple A Forum was due to the management's willingness to listen and act on comments and suggestions made and their approach to accessibility as a key part of their business plan – which aimed to make the O2 as open and usable as possible, by as many customers as possible. Members of the Triple A Forum had a wide range of personal experience of disability and provided expert comment on the centre's proposals. This inclusive engagement process and the management expectations and business perspective ensured that promoters working at the O2 complied with the access policy from the outset, providing a building, and services within the building, that are now very accessible. The way the Triple A Forum worked with management and the way management integrated accessibility and inclusion into their policies and practices resulted in the O2 achieving Gold status in the Attitude is Everything Charter of Good Practice.[19]

Not only were disabled people listened to and involved in the management decisions for the concert arena and the restaurant facilities, but access for disabled people was also achieved to the climb up over the roof of the O2 – 'Up at the O2'. Following advice from Neil Smith and David Dropkin, inclusive design consultants at BuroHappold, a passenger lift was installed to reach the starting platform and the design of the actual walkway over the roof, the equipment and the staff training all make it possible for wheelchair users to climb over the roof of the O2, alongside their family and friends, and enjoy the exhilarating experience and the amazing views over London from the very top (Figure 4.66). A bespoke wheelchair has been designed for use on the climb and a specialist team of four guides use a pulley system to help wheelchair users up and down.[20] There are, however, only a limited number of wheelchair-accessible climbs available as they can only take place in the spring and summer months, not when the weather is wet or windy – so there is a long waiting list.

The bespoke climbing shoes provided may not suit anyone who requires specific footwear, but the access forum is currently in discussion with the management regarding options for disabled people who have no choice but to wear their own footwear.

The approach to inclusive access is publicised well. There is detailed information on the main website providing advice on buying tickets and planning a visit prior to arrival, so you know how to get to and around the many different venues within the O2.[21] The information makes it clear that access is not just for wheelchair users – there is a Changing Places toilet, assistance dogs are welcome in all venues (water bowls are available), events are British Sign Language interpreted and audio described, and staff are on hand to help whenever needed.

Figure 4.66 **Louis Gorman (centre) was the first wheelchair user to climb over the roof of the O2 after the roof climb opened in 2012.**

5 Pancras Square, King's Cross, London

As part of its work to promote greater awareness of how to achieve an inclusive environment, the Construction Industry Council (CIC) runs an annual Inclusive Environment Award. Nominated in 2016 by the LABC (Local Authority Building Control), Camden Council was recognised by the CIC for going that extra mile beyond the minimum building regulation requirements in its provision of access for disabled people into and within its new headquarters building at 5 Pancras Square. This new office building, part of the redevelopment of the land behind King's Cross Station in London, is home to a leisure centre, library, café and a variety of council departments.

One of the particularly successful elements is the wayfinding scheme. The scale of the signs, their positioning, contrast and finishes, and the extensive use of pictograms has created a wayfinding system that is logical and intuitive, and the colour coding of the office floors brings a vibrancy to the building (Figures 4.67 and 4.68). A partially sighted member of staff frequently uses the colour coding to find her way around rather than having to rely on small numeric signs.

Wayfinding and design practice Whybrow, who designed the wayfinding scheme, worked closely with the client and the architects, Bennetts Associates, and produced a scheme that fully integrates with the architecture of the building. The atrium arrangement of the floor plate means that the bold, colourful floor-numbering system is visible throughout the building.

Figure 4.67 **5 Pancras Square, King's Cross, London, 2014 (Bennetts Associates [architects] and Whybrow [wayfinding scheme]): the colour-coded floor signs are clearly visible across the atrium, making finding your way around easy.**

Figure 4.68 **5 Pancras Square, King's Cross, London: the large, colourful floor-numbering signs are very easy to read.**

This adds to the experience and enjoyment of the building while being very informative, making it easy for visitors to find their way around – particularly important in an area where a high proportion of the population do not speak English as their first language. It has also helped to reinforce the council's vision for the new headquarters building to be open, helpful, supportive and modern.

Library of Birmingham

Winner of the Civic Trust Selwyn Goldsmith Award for Universal Design in 2015, the Library of Birmingham, designed by Mecanoo Architects with help from BuroHappold's Inclusive Design Team and Birmingham Access Committee, considered the needs of disabled people from the outset. Particularly striking are the Story Steps – an area set aside in the children's library to read and share stories (Figure 4.69). The bright yellow steps with bright red nosings help create an exciting space for children as well as demonstrating good accessibility.

Figure 4.69 **Library of Birmingham, 2013 (Mecanoo Architects): the red nosing on the bright yellow steps makes the children's Story Steps easy to use.**

Clink Street, Bankside, London

Uneven surfaces, particularly cobbles, can be very bumpy and uncomfortable, a 'jaw shattering experience' and even hazardous for some disabled and older people. (David Morris, the Mayor of London's disability policy advisor in 2008, described cobbles as 'the devil's pavement'.) But there is a solution – one of the schemes delivered to welcome disabled visitors to London for the London 2012 Olympic and Paralympic Games demonstrates how to respond to the use of cobbles in a historic setting. The Beijing Games in 2008 demonstrated its commitment to making the Games accessible to disabled people by installing a new passenger lift to the Great Wall of China, and the Athens Games in 2004 installed a new lift to give access to the Parthenon. London decided its demonstration project would be to make the Southbank Riverside Walk along the River Thames in London – a major tourist destination – accessible for disabled people. There were many locations along the walk where obstacles made access difficult or necessitated long detours. A total of £4 million was allocated by the government for the scheme, which included resurfacing Clink Street, one of the oldest medieval streets in London.

The original cobbles (although they were probably 20th Century, not actually medieval) were replaced by new granite setts in a colour palette – a variety of shades of white and grey – that echoed the historic character of the street (Figure 4.70). By working closely with English Heritage, an achievable solution was agreed – the sawn granite setts were closely jointed and laid to create a smooth, even surface. Clink Street is now enjoyed by thousands of tourists – disabled and non-disabled – who no longer risk being tripped up by the cobbles and can safely and comfortably enjoy the historic setting of the Clink Prison Museum and the remaining walls of Winchester Palace Great Hall, a Scheduled Ancient Monument, and its magnificent rose window on the west gable.

Figure 4.70 **Clink Street, Bankside, London, 2011 (Witherford Watson Mann Architects): the new granite setts, with a flat top and joints 13mm or less, have made one of London's oldest medieval streets smooth, level and easy to traverse.**

Tower Bridge, London

Another long-awaited improvement along the south bank of the River Thames, implemented in 2012, was the installation by the City of London Corporation of a passenger lift to the outside of Tower Bridge – a Grade I listed building. Designed by Sir John Wolfe Barry, the bridge opened to pedestrians and traffic in 1894. A dramatic addition to the London skyline, the bascule bridge, with high-level footbridges between twin stone towers, rises regularly to allow tall ships and vessels access to the upper reaches of the Pool of London. It also houses the Tower Bridge Exhibition. Prior to the lift being installed, anyone wanting step-free access from the exhibition gallery (which exits onto the bridge) to the engine rooms (which are entered from

Figure 4.71 **Passenger lift at Tower Bridge, London: the lift, installed by the City of London Corporation in 2012, provides step-free access from Tower Bridge down to the Thames Riverside Walk.**

the riverside walk), or indeed anyone walking along the bridge wanting to reach the riverside walk, had a very long detour down Tower Bridge Road to Horselydown Lane and over some very uneven cobbles. Today this passenger lift (Figure 4.71), located adjacent to the stairs, provides a quick and easy step-free route between the bridge and the riverside walk. It is very well used by everyone and demonstrates that a listed building can be altered sympathetically to create better access for all.

Beach Huts, Boscombe, Bournemouth

Bournemouth Council held an architectural competition in 2009 to design the first accessible beach hut in the UK. The £100,000 project was funded by Sea Change, a seaside cultural regeneration initiative by the Commission for Architecture and the Built Environment (CABE) to help regenerate seafronts. More than 170 competition entries were received, from as far afield as Chile, South Africa, China, Japan, North America and Europe. Residents, including local disabled people and Bournemouth DOTS Disability (the social enterprise arm of the charity Access Dorset), were asked to look at the scale models and illustrations and pick the winning design. The winning entry – 'Seagull and Windbreak' – was created by Peter Francis-Lewis and designed by ABIR Architects. Local disabled people provided advice and expertise throughout the design and build process. The two pairs of beach huts, located just west of Boscombe Pier, opened in 2011 (Figures 4.72 and 4.73). The flexible and adaptable design was recognised by the RIBA in 2012 with a regional award for Excellence in Architecture.

Figure 4.72 **Accessible Beach Huts, Boscombe Beach, Bournemouth, 2011 (ABIR Architects): these wheelchair-accessible beach huts provide much needed accessible facilities, as well as making a colourful addition to the seafront.**

The four accessible beach huts, with a floor area of 45sq m, replaced five standard beach huts. Each hut can accommodate four wheelchair users and the retractable partition walls enable two huts to be combined to create a larger unit for group hire. The huts are equipped with chairs, a table, a split-level work surface and kitchen units, a gas stove and a shared fresh drinking water tap.

The modern, colourful design is a great addition to the seafront, as well as providing facilities not just for wheelchair users but also for disabled and older people who need more space and more accessible facilities than the traditional beach hut allows.

The council's initiative to improve Boscombe Beach for disabled and older visitors also includes the provision of an electric charging point for mobility scooters, beach wheelchairs (on loan from Boscombe Beach Office), wheelchair-accessible public toilets, a Changing Places toilet with an overhead hoist and changing bed, Blue Badge parking bays and a wooden decked path made from beech wood to enable easy access onto the beach.[22]

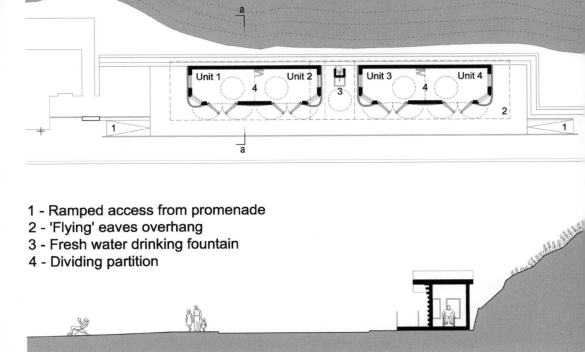

1 - Ramped access from promenade
2 - 'Flying' eaves overhang
3 - Fresh water drinking fountain
4 - Dividing partition

Figure 4.73 Accessible Beach Huts, Boscombe Beach, Bournemouth: this plan of the beach huts illustrates the flexibility of the space, which allows the huts to be used by groups as well as individuals.

The devil is in the detail

So far in this chapter we have looked at places that have been made accessible – in some cases despite seemingly impossible circumstances. That does not mean that those buildings are 'fully accessible', a phrase we like to use but is often impossible to achieve. Even in outwardly very accessible buildings, compromises in design detail are sometimes made to achieve a consensus at times of conflicting priorities. Even buildings that are very accessible and do not have complicated or conflicting priorities often have elements that don't work as well as they could for disabled people. So this section looks at common design pitfalls which can, with some forethought at the design stage, be easily overcome without increasing cost.

Tapering steps

A very common sight in the public realm – in new and old schemes – is the tapering step. Seen as a solution to a change in level on a sloping site, the tapering step creates irregular risers and narrowing treads, which can be hazardous to blind and partially sighted people who need to be able to place the whole foot on a step and for the risers to be uniform. With more and more of us walking around using our mobile phones instead of looking where we are going, this type of solution is becoming hazardous to everyone, not just blind and partially sighted people.

Placing seats or planting at the point where the step starts to taper and keeping the step risers and treads uniform can help to avoid this pitfall.

Often associated with tapering steps is a ramp that cuts through a flight of steps (Figures 4.74 and 4.75). Seen as a way of integrating access for those who need to use the ramp and those who need to use steps, this type of design in fact results in the creation of uneven risers and narrowing treads, along with the need to negotiate a crossfall where the ramp dissects the steps. Not only is this solution hazardous for blind and partially sighted people wishing to use the steps, but it also prevents the installation of an upstand and handrails on the ramp, potentially making the ramp hazardous for some users. Separating out the ramp from the steps makes negotiating the level change safer for everyone.

Figure 4.74 **This ramp at Peter's Hill, London, cuts through the steps, creating potentially hazardous tapering steps.**

Figure 4.75 **As well as the ramp cutting through the steps, there are no handrails on the steps, which also lack any contrast on the nosing. This makes both the steps and the ramp potentially hazardous, particularly for partially sighted people.**

Foreshortened handrails

Another common hazard for stair users is where the handrail stops short of the last step – more common on existing stairs than on new designs but still frequently seen. The horizontal extension of the handrail beyond the last step is helpful for all of us as it provides an indication that we are now on level ground, but is a critical clue for blind and partially sighted people. Being without a handrail while stepping down the last step can also be hazardous for older people who need support to the very end of the staircase.

A positive stop at the end of the handrail is also very helpful: returning the rail to the wall or having some sort of decorative end stops clothing getting caught in an open-ended rail, so is much safer and provides an additional clue to a blind person that the staircase has ended (Figures 4.76 and 4.77).

Figure 4.76 **This colourful object on a handrail in Portmeirion, in Wales, rather dramatically and obviously signals the end of the flight of stairs.**

Figure 4.77 **The inside of this handrail at the Asa Wright Centre in Trinidad is home to a tarantula – another good reason to ensure that the end of a handrail is closed and not left open!**

Figure 4.78 **Although these risers have been partially closed, feet can still get caught in the open section and many people find glass treads disconcerting and disorientating.**

Open step risers

Open risers in a staircase (often used when light is critical) are not good for many blind people and others who use a walking stick or who drag their feet. Sticks, feet and crutches can get stuck in the open risers and open risers have been advised against in the building regulations for over 20 years, yet they are still very common in modern buildings. The use of glass to close the riser is one solution, although not ideal as the light coming through the risers can sometimes cause disorientation (Figure 4.78).

Lack of contrast on step risers and treads

Another very common problem is where the edge of a step is indistinguishable from the tread of the step below. Highlighting the step nosing has also been in the building regulations for years and yet this detail is often overlooked, or poorly executed, even in brand-new stairs. The British Standard advises that a durable, permanently contrasting continuous material is incorporated into the step nosing for the full width of both the tread and the riser (Figure 4.79). A nosing that wraps around the tread for 50–65mm from the front edge of the tread and 30–55mm from the top of the riser will help to highlight the edge of the step and is particularly helpful to partially sighted people. The material should be slip resistant, firmly fixed and preferably matt so as not to induce glare. A common sight is a strip of carborundum set back from the edge of the step nosing, but as it does not wrap around the nosing it is not as visible as recommended, and inevitably the carborundum eventually starts to lift and becomes a trip hazard, so it is not recommended.

Figure 4.79 **The edges of these steps, at an office entrance in the City of London, are clearly highlighted.**

Figure 4.80 **Stainless-steel discs in the step edge can create glare and do not provide sufficient contrast to be helpful to partially sighted people.**

Using stainless steel or brass strips or studs along the tread is also common (Figure 4.80), but arguably does not provide a good enough contrast, particularly in strong sunlight, and it can be perceived to be slippery, so is not nearly as useful or as safe as a contrasting, matt non-slip nosing that wraps around the riser.

Stairs can be particularly hazardous and one of the major reasons for trips, slips and falls, often resulting in a serious injury. The safety of users, both inside a building and in the external environment, should be paramount, so the provision of a suitable nosing and handrail is critical. The surface of stairs is also crucial – the stair tread should be solid and slip resistant and with a consistent rise (for further detailed advice see Section 9.1 in BS 8300-1:2018).[23]

Narrow, uneven and cluttered paths

Even where footpaths are wide enough for two wheelchair users to pass or for a guide-dog user or a sign-language user to continue walking alongside a colleague (2m is the preferred minimum width), many common obstacles can still impede the journey (Figure 4.81). One of the most common hazards for blind and partially sighted people is plants and vegetation growing over the footway, cars parked on the pavement, low-level obstacles such as bollards below a metre in height, 'A' boards and other clutter outside shops and inconsistently located street furniture, adding up to a very difficult environment to negotiate.

Figure 4.81 Low bollards and an awkward camber make this street corner, in London, potentially hazardous.

Figure 4.82 **Located off the pedestrian desire line, this water feature, in Basinghall Street, in the City of London, is surrounded by tactile paving to warn blind and partially sighted people of the potential hazard, but is still an enjoyable and accessible feature.**

The removal of street clutter can be a real bonus, but it also has some unintended consequences. A common theme in street design today is to remove barriers from the footway at controlled crossings to allow more pedestrians to cross the road without being fenced in. This improves the flow of pedestrians in busy areas, but it can be a problem for people who find barriers and rails a useful leaning post while waiting for the traffic to stop or to take a rest.

Access can also be made difficult if street furniture or other physical elements are located on the main pedestrian desire line. Aligning street furniture – such as seats, bins, trees and planters – to one side of the pedestrian desire line can provide useful resting points as well as helping to delineate the clear, unobstructed footpath. For example, a water feature outside the Woolgate Exchange Building in Basinghall Street, London, is located slightly to one side of the main desire line from the footway to the building entrance to ensure it is not a hazard for blind or partially sighted pedestrians (Figure 4.82).

Seats without arms and back rests

Seats are an essential item of street furniture for many people and the lack of them, or their poor design, can make places no-go areas for some people. Benches without arms or back rests are not suitable for many disabled and older people – it can make standing up impossible. Some people who live with severe fatigue or constant pain benefit from public places where they can lie down, so benches are also useful, but should not be the only option.

Figure 4.83 **A seat with arms and a back rest is easier to use by people who need support when standing up or sitting down.**

Figure 4.84 **A place to lie down in public is useful for people who live with severe fatigue or constant pain.**

As per the principles of inclusive design, there should always be a choice of seating – some with arms and back rests, some without, but always at regular intervals (Figures 4.83 and 4.84).

Illegible wayfinding

A new section in the revised 2018 edition of BS 8300 provides advice on navigation, orientation and wayfinding. This is often not considered until the later stages of a project or as part of the signage contract, but the location of a building and its entrances on a site are critical if the optimum arrangement for easy, legible navigation and orientation are to be provided. A plethora of signs can often be as or more confusing than a lack of signs. So early consideration of the location of door entrances and exits in relation to taxi drop-off points, car parking, public transport arrival points and emergency egress, along with the provision of spatial physical and environmental clues, can help to make navigation easier.

Step-free access designed as the secondary route, not on the main desire line, can also make wayfinding difficult. Lifts remote from stairs can result in excessive travel distances for the very people who need travel distances to be kept to a minimum and can often mean that lift users have to cross large numbers of people going in a different direction. Where the location of the lift is not obvious or is remote from the main pedestrian desire line, you often see people precariously carrying a pushchair up the stairs. Locating all methods of vertical movement adjacent to each other provides an obvious choice and ensures easy, safe and quick movement for everyone, regardless of whether you are using a staircase, lift or escalator.

Wayfinding can be greatly assisted by providing a variety of ways to disseminate information. The tactile and audible map in Queen Elizabeth Olympic Park (see Chapter 3) provides both visual and audible information about the park's venues, making the map usable by blind people and deaf people. The pictures of the venues also make it accessible to children and people whose first language is not English (see Figure 4.85).

Figure 4.85 **This map of Queen Elizabeth Olympic Park is tactile and audible so accessible to a wide range of visitors and a good example of inclusive design.**

Heavy doors and confusing entrances

Once the building has been reached there are still many issues with the design of the entrance. Entrance doors are often indistinguishable from adjacent glazed walls and are too heavy to open to their full opening width. Manifestation is often ineffective, particularly in large areas of glazing where shadows, glare and reflections can disorientate, and is often placed only at adult height, not child height. Separate side doors located beside revolving doors are very often locked. The low section of a reception desk, designed to make wheelchair access easy, is often blocked by computers or even large bouquets of flowers! Where an induction loop has been installed, it often does not work and staff have not been trained in its use. Poor acoustics, highly patterned walls and a lack of contrast to highlight features can all make communicating with reception staff difficult. In contrast, using colour coding on doors can be beneficial (Figure 4.86).

Figure 4.86 **These colour-coded doors, at Portland College, Mansfield, are angled along the corridor to help students find the right room. The architects, Patel Taylor, won the RIBA CABE Inclusive Design Award in 2007.**

Highly patterned and shiny surfaces

Shiny or glossy floor surfaces, common in many high-end office developments, can disorientate and confuse even when not slippery, and pools of light on a shiny surface can appear like a pool of water – very disconcerting for someone with partial sight entering a building.

Highly patterned wall surfaces can make lip-reading difficult and using BSL very tiring, as can poor acoustics and hard surfaces that reverberate, design elements that should be considered in the design of entrance foyers, reception desks and conference and meeting rooms.

This chapter has given a flavour of some building elements that help create an accessible and inclusive environment, as well as some common design pitfalls that make access difficult. There are, of course, many other examples, both good and bad, that could have been included. Attention to detail can make all the difference between a place that is easy and comfortable to access and one that feels difficult or even unsafe to use. Advice to ensure that designs achieve accessibility and inclusivity is contained in BS 8300:2018 and should be essential reading for all built environment professionals.

As outlined in Chapter 1, design guidance, regulations and government policy have been promoting good inclusive design for years, yet the buildings that achieve award-winning inclusion are still the exception not the rule, and poorly detailed inaccessible designs are still very common. The next chapter looks at whether changes to legislation, policy and regulations would help to better enforce the implementation of best practice.

chapter 5

Towards better
legislation, policy
and regulations

'
Access, diversity and inclusion should be hard-wired through everything we do, not tucked away in human resources, not as part of corporate social responsibility, but hard-wired through every decision, every department, every process and every person.'

Speaker at the first Global Disability Innovation Hub Summit, July 2017

Despite some excellent examples of buildings and places that are very accessible, we have also seen in Chapter 4 some common pitfalls to accessible and inclusive design. But the lack of a handrail on a staircase or a heavy door can pale into insignificance in its effect on people's lives when compared to the difficulty of obtaining a suitable home, a job that is flexible enough to accommodate a fluctuating health condition or a workplace that is designed to enable you to reach your full potential. A quick trawl through some of the websites of organisations of disabled people gives a stark flavour of the difficulties many people still face today, despite years of planning policy, building regulation requirements and anti-discrimination legislation.

This chapter looks at whether the evolution of our legislation, regulations and technical standards (outlined in Chapter 1) has created a barrier to designing inclusively. It could be argued that the historical evolution of our approach – the 'special provision' route of amending the design to include a wheelchair user rather than designing to include the wheelchair user from the outset – has been 'normalised'. A different approach

– embracing inclusive design principles from the outset of every project – can make a real difference to people's lives. We seem happy to enact legislation, draft policy, improve standards and publish guidelines, but less enthusiastic about designing, building and enforcing high standards. This chapter looks at whether our current legislation, policy and regulations are fit for purpose and what can be done to elevate standards, accelerate change and ensure better implementation and more robust enforcement.

Improvements to legislation, policy and regulations can accelerate change

During the 1990s, a combination of anti-discrimination legislation and comprehensive building regulations seemed to be accepted as the way forward, not just in terms of the design of our buildings, places and spaces but also in helping to change society's attitude towards disabled people. Both were partly achieved by the millennium – the Disability Discrimination Act (DDA) was introduced in 1995 and the design standards in Approved Document M of the building regulations (Part M) were reviewed and improved in 1999 – and both contributed to accelerating change. Improvements continued into the 21st century. The DDA was revised when it was absorbed into the 2010 Equality Act (although some people believe, to maintain its status, it would have been better to retain the DDA rather than absorb it into the Equality Act, especially as certain aspects of the DDA, such as the requirement for reasonable adjustments, apply only to disabled people and not to people with the other characteristics protected by the Equality Act). Part M was further reviewed and amended in 2004, 2010, 2013 and again in 2015. Many buildings are considerably more accessible than they were 20 years ago, which could in part be attributed to legislation.

However, as was heard in the evidence given to the government's inquiry into Disability and the Built Environment in 2016, and as can be seen every day in our streets and buildings, any positive impact is still patchy and inconsistent across the country and across different building types, and people's lives continue to be restricted as a result.[1] To achieve our ambition of an accessible and inclusive environment, we need to recognise that the regulatory standards are still too limited and that there is inadequate enforcement of government policy, regulations and technical standards. If we are to make further progress, the first step is to strengthen legislation in relation to both new and existing buildings and public spaces. Improvements to the 2010 Equality Act, planning legislation and the building regulations could result in better implementation and more robust enforcement of good inclusive design. The government should also lead by example and send a positive message to the construction industry by ensuring that the highest standards of access and inclusion are a required and an explicit part of the procurement process in all government development and infrastructure projects.

Inclusive design is a critical element of planning policy
The impact of the effective application of robust planning policy is clear to see in the developments in and around Queen Elizabeth Olympic Park in east London (see Chapter 3).[2] Unfortunately, such robust planning policy is not ubiquitous across the country

and there are still many local authority local plans that do not effectively or explicitly address access for disabled people or inclusive design.

The Women and Equalities Select Committee recommended that no local plan should be found 'sound' by the planning inspectorate unless it has explicit policies on achieving an inclusive environment. The opportunity for the government to address this was provided with the revisions to the National Planning Policy Framework (NPPF) published in July 2018. However, reference to inclusive design and achieving an inclusive environment was not strengthened. The 2018 NPPF includes only one reference to inclusive design, in Paragraph 127, which states that planning policies and decisions should ensure that developments:

create places that are safe, inclusive and accessible and which promote health and well-being, with a high standard of amenity for existing and future users; and where crime and disorder, and the fear of crime, do not undermine the quality of life or community cohesion and resilience.[3]

It could be argued that this is all that is needed to make local planning authorities incorporate robust policies in their local plans. Yet experience has demonstrated that this is not the case. The Planning Inspectorate should now increase its efforts to make sure that paragraph 127f of the NPPF is properly enforced and that plans are not passed unless they include clear, explicit and robust policies on accessible and inclusive design.

No mention is made in the NPPF of the need to address access and inclusion at the outset of every project – at master plan and outline brief stages. One way to accelerate change is for local plans to include policy that makes this an explicit requirement of all major development proposals.

The opportunity to be more robust on the design of new homes was also lost. Although the use of the optional accessible housing standards contained within the building regulations is included, it is only a footnote to paragraph 127f, not within the main body of the text, where it would have had more impact. The footnote states:

> Planning policies for housing should make use of the Government's optional technical standards for accessible and adaptable housing, where this would address an identified need for such properties. Policies may also make use of the nationally described space standard, where the need for an internal space standard can be justified.[4]

Some simple administrative changes, such as a standard question on planning application forms that requires applicants to explain how their scheme addresses inclusive access for disabled people, would also highlight to developers and planning applicants that accessible and inclusive design is an essential element of any scheme. The application form should also require applicants to state how many accessible and adaptable or wheelchair-user dwellings will be provided within the scheme. This would also assist local planning authorities in collating data and monitoring these elements. Further advice on the content of access statements submitted with planning applications would also help.

Improving the building regulations

Planning policies, such as those in the London Plan and in the London Legacy Development Corporation's Local Plan, would seem on the surface to be enough to ensure inclusive access is implemented (Figure 5.1). However, given that the government first made access for disabled people a planning matter back in 1981, when the Disabled Persons Act introduced Section 29A and Section 29B into the 1971 Town and Country Planning Act, the answer must be no! That is not to say that planning policy isn't an essential and critical tool to deliver accessible and inclusive buildings and spaces, but on its own it is not enough.

Even with robust planning polices, the scheme must successfully make its way through the building control process. Part M of the building regulations, despite considerable improvement over the years, only sets minimum standards needed to achieve a basic level of accessibility – it is a safety net rather than the standard to aim for, hence the London Plan policy asking for the highest standards of access and inclusion not the minimum.[5] (See Chapter 1 for details of London Plan policies.)

As well as an amendment to make Changing Places WCs mandatory in large public buildings (see Chapter 1), the building regulations should be reviewed to amend the requirements for accessible housing. Planning policy for M4(3) may be the appropriate vehicle to address the provision of wheelchair-user housing, but the requirements of M4(2) (similar to the original Lifetime Home standard) should be made a mandatory requirement of Part M for all new homes, rather than relying on local planning authority local plan policies, which can lead

Figure 5.1 This graphic, from Accessible London, the Greater London Authority's Supplementary Planning Guidance to the 2011 London Plan, illustrates that inclusive design is not a minority issue but benefits everyone.

to inappropriate geographical variations in the provision of accessible housing. Where it is impossible to provide step-free access as required by M4(2), for example a flat above a shop or garage, the access statement process can be used to explain the particular circumstances of the case.

The non-domestic section of Approved Document M (Volume 2) should also be reviewed and updated. It has improved compared to 20 years ago, but it is still a long way from addressing the comprehensive standards in British Standard Code of Practice BS 8300 – the most recent 2018 revisions now include more than 300 pages of technical advice and guidance.

Given the increasing understanding and knowledge of how to design buildings and places that reduce levels of anxiety and create more comfortable and safer places for people with autism, dementia, neuro-diverse conditions and mental health issues, consideration should also now be given to incorporating appropriate design requirements into Part M. Advice on wayfinding and orientation, better use of colour and contrast in external and internal environments, acoustics that support the interpretation of sound and speech, and illumination levels that provide a safe and comfortable environment are all areas which could be further considered for inclusion in the next iteration of Part M.

At the time of writing, the independent inquiry into the horrific fire at Grenfell Tower on 14 June 2017 is ongoing. A substantial amount of work is also being undertaken by the construction industry in response to the tragedy and in response to the issues raised by Dame Judith Hackitt in her Independent Review of

Building Regulations and Fire Safety.[6] The government has started a programme of work to bring about a fundamental change to the regulations to ensure that residents of high-rise buildings are safe and feel safe. Access and egress for disabled and older people in new and existing buildings will be impacted by this, but it is not possible to comment further at this stage.

Inclusive Design Strategies built into project briefs and procurement processes

> More rigour and oversight at the front end of the process can lead to significant increases in productivity, reduction in ongoing costs and to better outcomes for all in the later and ongoing stages of the process. Improving the procurement process will play a large part in setting the tone for any construction project. This is where the drive for quality and good outcomes, rather than lowest cost, must start.'
>
> Dame Judith Hackitt, Building a Safer Future report, 2018[7]

The inclusion and better enforcement of robust planning policy in local plans, along with improvements to the technical standards in the building regulations, will help to ensure inclusive access is properly considered at planning stage and effectively implemented at building control stage. But to make these tools work more effectively we need to create a system that ensures clients, developers and contractors consider accessibility from the outset of any project. Inclusive design principles should be integrated into the development process from the very beginning and their implementation monitored throughout the procurement, design, planning, construction and completion stages. The way the building or service is managed once occupied should also be monitored and regularly reviewed. We saw in Chapter 3 the significant impact that addressing accessibility issues in the procurement, tendering and budgetary processes can have on delivering good inclusive design (rather than relying solely on planning and building control to address accessibility). So it is very helpful that BS 8300 now includes advice on the importance of addressing access and inclusion from the outset of any project. Addressing inclusive design principles in a master plan and at outline planning application stage can help to maximise accessibility and is a critical part of the inclusive development process, but BS 8300:2018 goes further and recommends, in Section 4, that the development of an Inclusive Design Strategy forms part of the strategic vision (see Table 1 in BS 8300-2:2018), with the principles of inclusive design embedded into the initial concept brief. It advises that budget estimates, procurement processes and development agreements should make explicit reference to meeting best practice, helping to establish the principles of an inclusive development prior to the drafting of master plans and outline designs.

The Construction Industry Council has reiterated these principles in its Essential Principles Guide for Clients, Developers and Contractors: Creating an Accessible and Inclusive Environment.[8] Table 5.1 illustrates when and how in the development process inclusive design principles should be applied.

Inclusive Design Strategy

Strategic vision	Commit to implementing an inclusive design process and identify an Inclusive Environment Champion.
Initial concept brief	Embed the principles of inclusive design into the brief.
Budget estimates	Structure the budget to ensure that costs address accessibility and inclusivity, including costs of access expertise on the project team from inception to completion.
Procurement process	Incorporate the principles of inclusive design into procurement requirements.
Development agreements	Make explicit reference to meeting best practice standards in any development agreements.
Master plan and outline designs	Initiate early consultation and engagement with strategic user groups, including local access groups and groups of people with characteristics protected by the 2010 Equality Act.
Planning application	Use Design and Access Statements to demonstrate how the highest standards of access and inclusion have been achieved.
Building control application	Demonstrate in any Access Strategy how access solutions have met the vision of an inclusive environment.

Detailed design and product selection	Maintain vigilance in the detailed design and project selection to ensure that inclusive access and facilities are delivered.
Construction phase	Ensure that value engineering or other changes during the construction phase are not to the detriment of inclusive design or accessibility – attention to detail is critical.
Appraisal at project completion	Audit accessibility and means of escape provisions prior to completion using access expertise.
Fit out and post occupancy evaluation	Maintain levels of accessibility and ensure that staff are fully trained in the use of facilities.
In-use management policies, practices and procedures	Monitor future changes and embed the principles of inclusive design into planned maintenance programmes.
Long-term occupancy, end user/ public feedback	Review end-user feedback, tailored audit changes and customer surveys, and use lessons learned to enhance inclusive design in future projects.

Table 5.1 **Inclusive Design Strategy**[9]

Developers of major schemes, especially government-funded major developments, should adopt this practice as a normal part of the development process. Addressing accessibility issues in the procurement, tendering and budgetary processes, not relying solely on the planning and building control process to address accessibility can have a significant impact on delivering good inclusive design.

In December 2017 the government's National Infrastructure and Construction Pipeline contained projections of £600 billion of public and private investment in infrastructure over the next 10 years.[10] The National Infrastructure Delivery Plan set out the government's plans to support the delivery of housing, and social and economic infrastructure, across the public and private sectors, including £117 billion in social infrastructure.[11] This surely provides a huge opportunity to design and build new infrastructure that demonstrates best practice in accessible and inclusive design. The government should lead by example and ensure that all government contracts are dependent on an inclusive development process, tied in to contracts as part of procurement and assessed as part of any tendering process.

Leading by example and making inclusion mandatory in all government infrastructure and development contracts will also help to encourage developers, clients and building owners to achieve inclusion in privately funded developments. All large private sector developments should be encouraged through government policy to adopt a similar approach.

Opportunities through licensing legislation

Another opportunity to improve access and facilities for disabled people is when premises are licensed (for entertainment, wedding and civil partnership ceremonies and the sale of alcohol). However, the licensing legislation does not currently influence whether a licensed premises is accessible or not – relying on service providers to abide by the requirements of the 2010 Equality Act. An opportunity to embed accessibility requirements into the legislation was missed when the Marriage Act was introduced in 1994 and local authorities were required to approve premises for wedding ceremonies.

Some local authorities do use the wedding licence application process to encourage the provision of improved access and facilities for disabled people. The City of London Corporation building control officers, on their site visit to assess the means of escape provision, are accompanied by the access advisor, who assesses the level of accessibility for disabled people and provides advice to the applicant as part of the formal licence application process. Consideration is given to whether the following has been provided:

- at least one parking space reserved for Blue Badge holders (where on-site parking is provided)
- an accessible entrance into the property from the public footway and parking area
- an accessible route through the building to the room(s) where the marriage ceremonies are to be conducted and any associated function rooms
- a wheelchair-accessible toilet
- a hearing induction loop or other hearing enhancement facility in the marriage ceremony room.[12]

Many venues have heeded the advice and improved their facilities, helping to ensure that access is available to disabled people in many wedding venues within the Square Mile. The Corporation cannot, however, enforce changes to the provision of access or facilities for disabled people, it can only advise, so relies on the licensee to recognise the economic and social benefits of good accessibility, and their duties under the Equality Act, which sadly is not always the case.

Other types of licences, such as alcohol and entertainment licences, could also be used to ensure that pubs, clubs and restaurants become more accessible. Many campaigns have been run over the years to get the licensing laws changed. The latest success is in Scotland, where the Barred! campaign has achieved a change in the law so that licence applicants must publish information on how accessible their premises are to disabled people. The Licensing (Scotland) Act 2005: Guidance for Completing A Disabled Access and Facilities Statement came into force in March 2018 following an eight-year campaign by Edinburgh wheelchair user Mark Cooper.[13] Frustrated and angry that his favourite pubs did not have accessible toilets, he began campaigning for a change in the law which would force publicans to declare, when applying for a drinks licence, how accessible their premises were for disabled users. However, although the Act requires applicants to publish an access statement (helping disabled people find an accessible pub and raising licensees' awareness), it does not require the venue to be made accessible to disabled people – it still relies on the individual disabled person to take a case under the 2010 Equality Act if provision has not been reasonably made. This is another lost opportunity to use the licensing laws to help enforce good inclusive design.

To speed up access improvements in these types of premises, consideration should be given to how licensing or other appropriate legislation could be amended, so that applicants for wedding, alcohol and entertainment licences are required to assess the accessibility of their premises and make reasonable adjustments and physical alterations to allow disabled and older people to access and use the facility or service being licensed.

Inclusive design is sustainable design

Inclusion is the absolute enabler of real sustainable innovation.'

Speaker at the first Global Disability Innovation Hub Summit, July 2017

Sustainable development has been a key government policy in the UK for years and is now a key element of most new developments. Sustainability does, of course, embrace three distinct dimensions – economic, environmental and social. However, the environmental element tends to be the main focus in the construction industry, with the industry spending much less time considering the social aspects. To compound this, inclusive design is still seen as a social issue not an economic or environment issue – yet a building, place or space is not sustainable if it is not accessible and inclusive.

Goal 11 of the United Nations (UN) Sustainable Development Goals recognises that inclusivity is integral to achieving sustainable cities and communities, and the UN has stressed the critical role disabled people play as invaluable partners in achieving the 2030 Agenda for Sustainable Development. The UN's eighth Secretary-General, Ban Ki-moon, said, 'Let us work together for a world of opportunity and dignity for all, a future of inclusion, one in which we all gain by leaving no one behind.'[14]

Implementing the new Sustainable Development Goals for all disabled people is now a focus of those governments signed up to the Convention on the Rights of Persons with Disabilities. Yet it is debatable how much the need to create an inclusive environment is recognised by those with a sustainability focus.

More effective use of BRE's Environmental Assessment Method (BREEAM) would help to change this approach. BREEAM is the world's most widely used environmental assessment method for buildings and sets the standard for best practice in sustainable design. BREEAM ratings have made a huge difference to how developers respond to the need to make their buildings energy efficient and meet other environmental requirements. But how much attention is paid to the sections that address inclusive design? The BREEAM Communities Technical Manual, in its social and economic wellbeing section, considers societal and economic factors affecting health and wellbeing, such as inclusive design, cohesion, adequate housing and access to employment.[15] The criteria are not mandatory but are nevertheless very helpful in raising the access and inclusivity issue at an early stage in the development process. Encouraging clients to achieve all three credits will help to better embed inclusive design into projects.

BREEAM Communities Technical Manual 2012: SE 15 Inclusive Design

Aim

To create an inclusive community by enhancing accessibility for as many current and future residents as possible.

Assessment criteria

The following is required to demonstrate compliance:

One credit

1 An inclusive design and operational management strategy is produced at the outset of the development including issues of accessibility, inclusion and emergency egress for all occupants and visitors, with specific consideration to people's wellbeing, age, gender, ethnicity, beliefs and/or disability related needs.

2 Consultation and recognised national and local guidance are used to inform inclusive design and operational management.

Two credits

3 Criteria 1 to 2 are achieved.

4 An individual person is appointed within the design team to champion and provide oversight on inclusive design during the development of the master plan.

5 The master plan incorporates relevant aspects of inclusive design.

Three credits

6 Criteria 1 to 5 are achieved.

7 An appropriately qualified independent access consultant is appointed to provide expert advice on both the strategic and detailed design proposals.

8 The independent access consultants' recommendations have been incorporated into the master plan and used to inform operational management strategy.[16]

To help embed this further into sustainability practice, the BREEAM New Construction 2018 standard states that the minimum consultation content of the consultation plan should typically include 'implementing principles and processes that deliver an inclusive and accessible design' and in transportation hubs it should 'recognise the diversity of user needs, including people of all ages and abilities' (MAN 01 Project Brief and Design).[17]

Another UN initiative – the New Urban Agenda – aims to readdress the way cities are planned, designed, financed, developed, governed and managed. One of the aims is to promote inclusive and sustainable economic growth. The needs of disabled people are recognised and highlighted throughout the commitments made by those governments signing the agenda. The challenge now is to address and implement these commitments effectively.

Existing, historic and listed buildings can be made accessible

The age and nature of our towns and cities, developed over centuries, is often blamed for the lack of easy access, yet improvements can and should be undertaken. The proportion of buildings replaced each year stands at only 1 per cent, so there are a substantial number of existing, historic and listed buildings with poor accessibility. Adapting existing buildings to make them accessible is not always easy and can be expensive but there are usually solutions. Many people still assume that if a building is listed or in a conservation area it cannot be made accessible. However, many existing and listed buildings have successfully been made accessible while respecting their character and their historic nature.

English Heritage (now called Historic England) published advice on improving access to historic buildings and historic landscapes back in 2004. Both guidance documents were updated in 2014 and 2015. The documents provide clear advice, stating:

Too many people think of the historic environment as being inaccessible. Historic England knows that this need not be the case. On the contrary, we know that good quality access can enhance our understanding of the historic environment and ensure its sustainability. What we have learnt is that with the right kind of thought and discussion a way can be found round almost any barrier.[18]

In its information on how to comply with the law, Historic England explains the relationship between duties not to discriminate enshrined in the 2010 Equality Act and the planning and listed building legislation:

It is important in principle that everyone should have dignified access to and within historic buildings to which the Act applies. If treated as part of an integrated review of access arrangements for all visitors or users and a flexible and pragmatic approach is taken, it should normally be possible to plan suitable access for disabled people or others with a protected characteristic without compromising a building's special interest. Alternative routes or reorganising the use of space may achieve the desired result without the need for damaging alterations.[19]

Chester, one of England's most historic towns, won the European Commission's Access City Award in 2017, demonstrating that even a city with a large number of listed buildings, two miles of Roman walls and fortifications and a historic shopping centre on two levels (called The Rows) can still be made accessible (Figures 5.2 and 5.3).[20]

Owners of historic and listed buildings and other heritage assets, along with local authorities who implement the listed building legislation, can learn from examples of good practice and should encourage and implement innovative and creative ways to improve access for disabled people to existing buildings. Environmental improvement schemes, health and wellbeing initiatives, using the power of town centre managers and the influence of business improvement districts could all help to accelerate the achievement of an accessible environment.

Figure 5.2 **A number of level and ramped access points provide step-free access to The Rows in Chester.**

Figure 5.3 **Ramps make Chester's Roman walls accessible.**

The need for more accessible and adaptable housing

> '
> More than 90 per cent of older people in England
> live in mainstream housing, as opposed to specialist
> housing or residential care. However, current UK
> housing stock is often not accessible or adapted to
> meet people's needs as they get older, with small
> room sizes, steep internal stairs, baths rather than
> showers and steps outside.'
>
> Centre for Ageing Better, Room to Improve, 2017 [21]

The English Housing Survey has estimated that there are at least
475,000 households in England that include adults over the age
of 65 who live with a disability or long-term limiting illness and who
report that they lack the home adaptations they need.[22] This is
likely to be an underestimate as the number of older people who
would benefit from adaptations is probably considerably higher.

Over 30 years ago it was recognised that designing general-needs
housing that was accessible and easily adaptable (as opposed to
'special for the disabled' wheelchair-accessible housing) would
provide much-needed homes for a wide range of households,
including for many older and disabled people. As far back as 1978
the British Standards Institution published a code of practice (called
Design of Housing for the Convenience of Disabled People) with
provisions for ensuring that ordinary new housing was convenient
for disabled people to live in or visit. This was promoted throughout
the 1980s and by 1989 the Helen Hamlyn Foundation coined
the phrase Lifetime Homes – homes that would maximise 'utility,

independence and quality of life' when considering the needs of older people. Joining with Habinteg Housing Association, the Joseph Rowntree Foundation, the Access Committee for England and others to form the Lifetime Homes Group, this culminated in the publication of the Lifetime Homes standards in 1993.[23] It has gone through various iterations since then, including being the basis for the British Standard Code of Practice BS 9266:2013,[24] but it wasn't until 2016 that these standards, in a modified form, were included as Part M4(2) of the building regulations. Furthermore, as explained earlier, M4(2) is currently only an optional standard, which can be applied to a development only if 'switched on' locally by adopted planning policy requirements.

It is no surprise then that the Equality and Human Rights Commission (EHRC) report Housing and Disabled People: Britain's Hidden Crisis highlighted a continuing lack of accessible housing provided by local authorities and registered landlords, preventing many disabled people living independently. Only 7 per cent of homes offer minimal accessibility features. The report found that the impact of unsuitable housing on disabled people is particularly acute and that:

- disabled people are too often demoralised and frustrated by the housing system
- there is a significant shortage of accessible homes
- installing home adaptations involves unacceptable bureaucracy and delay
- disabled people are not getting the support that they need to live independently.[25]

Campaigns like Leonard Cheshire Disability Home Truths demonstrate the difficulty disabled people have in finding suitable housing – one in six disabled adults and half of all disabled children live in housing that isn't suitable for their needs.[26] The video clips on the EHRC website illustrate with real-life stories the frustration and difficulties many disabled people are experiencing.

The EHRC report recommended that the UK government:

- introduces a national strategy to ensure there is an adequate supply of new houses built to inclusive design standards and to wheelchair-accessible standards, across all tenures

- amends requirement M4(2) of Schedule 1 to the Building Regulations 2010 so it is no longer an optional requirement, but becomes the default and mandatory minimum standard for the design and delivery of all new homes

- mandates that all local authorities ensure a minimum of 10 per cent of new-build houses across all tenure types are built to M4(3) standard, the higher wheelchair-accessible standards.[27]

The EHRC report is not the only recent report to look at the impact that the lack of accessible housing is having on the lives of disabled people. The House of Commons Select Committee on Housing, Communities and Local Government, in its 2018 report on housing for older people, examined whether the housing on offer for older people is sufficiently available and suitable for their needs, and at how older people wish to live.[28] The report recommended that all new homes should be built to accessible and adaptable standards so they are 'age proofed' and can meet the current and future needs of older people.

This would help overcome one of today's challenges, helping to respond to people's changing housing needs and preferences as they grow older and want to make changes to the way they live. The Centre for Ageing Better recently reported on the benefits that small-scale adaptations can bring about, improving people's lives.[29] The more accessible your home is to start with, the easier it will be to adapt it to your changing needs.

Although there is an increasing number of well-designed specialist housing schemes for older people, a lot of older people do not want to move into specialist housing.[30] Unfortunately, the housing industry has been slow to recognise the growing market of older people wishing to downsize into a home that is spacious, accessible and easily adaptable. Owners of public and commercial buildings are increasingly recognising the value of accessible buildings and are including this more frequently in their audits of buildings prior to purchase. They are also recognising that it is cheaper to build in access from the start, as the cost of adaptations and making reasonable adjustments once a building is occupied can be far higher. A home that is already accessible also reduces the likelihood of the occupant needing long, unnecessary hospital stays while suitable and often expensive adaptions are undertaken. The unnecessary cost that 'bed blocking' is placing on the NHS is gradually being recognised. If the housing industry followed the commercial market and started to recognise the added value of accessible housing by building in easy access from the outset, this could help to transform the lives of many disabled and older people and families with small children – a benefit for all of us.

The drive towards healthy streets

Even when we live in homes designed to meet our needs, as soon as we venture outside our front doors the design, management and facilities available in the public realm can make our ability to work, play, shop or visit friends and family difficult and sometimes impossible. The Healthy Streets Approach adopted by the Mayor of London aims to improve health and reduce health inequalities by making changes to the character and use of streets and so increase the number of people who choose to walk, cycle and use public transport.[31] Ten indicators are used to reflect the experience of being on the streets:

- clean air
- pedestrians from all walks of life
- easy to cross
- shade and shelter
- places to stop and rest
- not too noisy
- people choose to walk, cycle and use public transport
- people feel safe
- things to see and do
- people feel relaxed.

Delivering improvements that support these indicators can help disabled and older people – and everyone – access and use our streets and the spaces between buildings more easily and comfortably.

Two particular issues – the lack of public toilet facilities (of all sizes and designs) and the fashion for introducing 'shared space' schemes in busy streets – can have a significant impact on how people use and experience the public realm. These are areas where change could have a significant impact on the inclusivity of our streets.

One of the major issues facing disabled and older people when away from home is the lack of suitable and available public toilet facilities. Many studies have been undertaken making this point time and time again.[32] Having closed down many of the Victorian public toilets located in our streets and parks, some local authorities have introduced a community toilet scheme, whereby they pay a restaurant or pub a small sum to allow the public to use their toilet facilities for free.[33] However, this has not provided the service needed and is not the solution. It is not always easy to find a WC in the back of a crowded pub or busy restaurant, they may not be accessible to disabled people and of course they will only be available during opening times, so not as easily available as WCs on a street.

The Mayor of London's draft London Plan has recognised the importance of publicly accessible toilet facilities and has included a policy on their provision (see overleaf).

This is laudable and will make a difference in some areas and can be good for business – as noted in the supporting text, the availability of public toilets will benefit the night-time economy. However, particularly in areas where there is little new large-scale commercial development, this will still leave vast areas

The London Plan: Draft for Public Consultation, December 2017

Policy S6 Public toilets

Development proposals that include large-scale developments that are open to the public, such as shops, sport, leisure and health care facilities, transport hubs, cultural and civic buildings, and large areas of public realm, should provide and secure the future management of free publicly accessible toilets. These should be available during opening hours, or 24 hours a day in areas of public realm and should be suitable for a range of users including disabled people, families with young children and people of all gender identities.[34]

of our towns and cities with insufficient provision, particularly for disabled people. Although it is difficult in times of financial austerity, the government should re-introduce the statutory duty for local authorities to provide public toilet facilities in public places.

The other major issue in the public realm and another area which has been extensively written about and criticised is the recent introduction of 'shared space' designs, where features such as kerbs, road surface markings, designated crossing places and traffic signs are removed. A concept introduced from the Netherlands more than 10 years ago, it has been severely criticised by Guide Dogs (the UK charity for blind and partially sighted people) and the Royal National Institute of Blind People.

Street designs that slow traffic speeds, reduce clutter, widen footways and strengthen pedestrian priority are, of course, very beneficial to everyone. However, many 'shared space' designs introduce a shared surface where the kerb is removed, and the road and pavement are built at the same level, so that cars, buses, cyclists and pedestrians use and share the same surface and are expected to negotiate use of the space by making eye contact. Even where a tactile strip of paving has been installed as a warning between the carriageway and the footway, for many blind and partially sighted people, for children taught to stop at the kerb before crossing, and for those of us used to the traditional division between the carriageway and the footway, the removal of a kerb can be very confusing, difficult to navigate and even hazardous.

Despite the best efforts of the access group set up to advise on the proposals, the Exhibition Road scheme in Kensington, London, has come in for a lot of criticism. Although the scheme has significantly widened the footway on the west side, considerably improving pedestrian access into the museums and so a welcome improvement, the lack of a traditional kerb combined with the large amount of busy traffic using the street has made some blind people feel vulnerable using the street, often taking action to avoid using it at all.

The Chartered Institution of Highways and Transportation (CIHT), in its industry review of shared space, called Creating Better Streets, made a number of recommendations to industry and local authorities. The recommendations include:

- the need for greater awareness to create streets that are inclusive and accessible
- the development and use of a framework of objectives and outcomes for the basis of street design
- the need to replace the use of shared space as a concept with different design approaches
- the need for detailed research into the needs of all users and around specific design features
- the review of existing guidance and the development of new guidance to assist local authorities in producing better street design
- consideration of amending legislation in certain areas.[35]

Lord Holmes of Richmond was critical of the dangers that some shared space schemes presented to blind and partially sighted people but was positive about the report saying:

I am delighted that the recommendations include ensuring that local authorities understand their duties with regard to the Equality Act and also recognise that greater awareness, better training, more research and improved guidance are all needed.

I'm also delighted that the report concludes – regarding crossings – that 'there should be sufficient provision for all users to cross the carriageway safely and in comfort' and – regarding kerbs – that the separation between carriageway and footway 'should be clearly delineated and detectable by all'. It is essential that all our public spaces are safe, inclusive places for us all to enjoy.[36]

The Department for Transport requested in 2018 that local authorities paused introducing any further shared space schemes until further research is undertaken, and advice reviewed and updated. Their Inclusive Transport Strategy stressed: 'It is for local authorities to ensure any pedestrian environment scheme, including a shared space, is inclusive and that they meet the requirements of the Equality Act 2010'.[37] It remains to be seen how quickly the research is completed, how far the revised guidance addresses the need for a clearly delineated and detectable separation between the carriageway and the footway, and how effectively local authorities implement the revised advice.

A better way to challenge disability discrimination

The 2010 Equality Act is an essential tool for disabled people to use to ensure provision of equal and fair access to buildings and services, but it is clearly failing in its original aim if too many places are still inaccessible. A better and easier way needs to be found to require building owners and service providers to make inaccessible existing buildings and services accessible. It is unreasonable to expect disabled people to continually take cases under the Equality Act to make their local pub or restaurant or other places of entertainment accessible – one complaint to the local authority should be all that is needed by the individual and the case should then be taken up by the council. The Act places the responsibility to challenge the design of a building onto the individual disabled person. In contrast, other consumer rights, including complaints about noise and about food and hygiene in restaurants, are investigated by Environmental Health and Trading Standards officers. If a restaurant is failing in its duties under the food and hygiene regulations, a customer can ask the local authority to investigate, and the local authority can then serve notice to resolve the issue. If a restaurant is failing in its duty to provide a service to a disabled person by, for example, not providing an accessible toilet or by preventing use of that toilet by using the space as a storeroom, the only course of action is to make a personal complaint of discrimination under the Equality Act. Not many people want to spend time taking every inaccessible restaurant, shop or service provider to court. A more effective way to ensure equal access would be to change the legislation so that complaints about lack of access and facilities are addressed by the local authority.

Another barrier is the cost of taking a discrimination case through the courts, the reduction in legal aid, and the fact that many disabled people are unaware of their rights and how to enforce them. Those cases that are settled are often settled out of court so are confidential and information cannot be put into the public domain. Law firms such as Fry Law are, however, starting to upload onto their website information about the discrimination cases they are working on, to try to publicise cases and demonstrate the wide variation of services that are being successfully challenged.

A review of enforcement of the Equality Act was launched by the Women and Equalities Select Committee in July 2018.[38] Questions included whether the introduction of a duty on local authorities to investigate complaints made by a disabled person about the lack of access and facilities in premises where a public service is provided would help to make many more buildings accessible. Time will tell whether the evidence submitted is sufficient to result in amendments to the legislation and whether additional resources will be made available to local authorities to effectively implement any new duties.

Towards better implementation

Legislation, government policy and the development of best practice standards in the UK have led to much greater accessibility, but barriers continue to exist so we cannot be complacent. We need to continually review the effectiveness of legislation, policy and best practice standards and assess the need to make further improvements. Requiring inclusive access strategies at procurement and tendering stages, reinforcing that inclusive access is a planning matter (as it has been for over 30 years), improving the building regulations and changing equality legislation to enable more effective ways of challenging discrimination in building design and service provision will all contribute to improving the inclusivity of our buildings, places and spaces.

However, good legislation or improved regulation does not necessarily mean good implementation or effective enforcement – this is one area where government initiatives should be driving further change.

The next chapter looks at how our attitudes and our behaviour towards implementing best practice are gradually changing, but also at how our knowledge and skills need to improve and how, as part of our ethical and professional code of practice, every built environment professional should take responsibility for aiming to achieve the highest standards of inclusion.

chapter **6**

**Towards
an inclusive
future**

> My vision is for a world in which designers, architects and artists treat access requirements as creative opportunities rather than clunky bolt-on afterthoughts.'
>
> Speaker at the first Global Disability Innovation Hub Summit, July 2017

The last chapter looked at how updating legislation, policy and regulations would help to better implement and enforce higher standards of inclusive design. This chapter looks at whether architectural and environmental barriers to inclusion continue to persist because of our attitude, our behaviour, our lack of knowledge and skills, and a resistance to understanding and responding to difference. Architects, designers, planners – most built environment professionals – can and do play a critical role in creating inclusive buildings and places, as do clients, developers and building owners. By looking at our own attitude towards disability, health and difference we can start to dismantle some of the barriers to achieving inclusion.

We all have our own experiences of environmental, economic and social barriers, whether we identify as a disabled person or not, but if we lack any real understanding of how people different to ourselves perceive, use and experience buildings and spaces we will fail to design inclusively. A wheelchair user will not understand how a blind person experiences a building any more than someone who doesn't use a wheelchair, unless they spend the time learning about and understanding those experiences. Engaging effectively with people with a variety of lived experience of architectural and environmental barriers can provide an essential understanding of how to design and build to include. Effective engagement can be difficult, especially where budgets are restricted, when it can become tokenistic, but working with different communities can expand knowledge and is one of the most effective ways of ensuring better inclusion in a scheme. Establishing access panels at the outset of a project, whose views are listened to and incorporated into the design and development of the project, is very effective. Co-production (local residents working together with decision makers) can be even more successful at ensuring full engagement, as well as empowering the local community.

Improving our knowledge and skills and learning to embrace inclusion and diversity seem fundamental to dismantling the physical barriers that already exist. Recognising that we need to continually expand our knowledge, skills and understanding of how to design for inclusion is key. An increasing number of initiatives are looking at new ways of teaching, learning and practising the art of inclusive design – some are highlighted here.

Knowing the cost of what we are missing out on by not being inclusive – the skills a diverse workforce brings to an organisation, as well as the financial benefits of a wider customer base – is also a powerful argument. The chapter ends by looking at how to encourage clients to embrace an inclusive design approach and how we can all help to change mind-sets and behaviours, become inclusive designers and look forward to an inclusive future.

Changing our behaviour

How can we make ourselves more aware of the processes and prejudices that make us not listen?'

Mary Beard, Women and Power: A Manifesto, 2017[1]

We have heard many messages from different governments and local authorities over the years who have been determined to eradicate disability discrimination and to create an accessible and inclusive built environment. Yet, despite significant improvements, there is an obvious disconnect between these statements, policies and intentions and reality. Discrimination still exists and continues to prevent many disabled people from fulfilling their ambitions and desires because of the way we continue to build new and maintain old barriers to inclusive access in our buildings, places and spaces. This can, in part, be attributed to our attitude towards disability and our inability to see disabled people as ourselves.

Rob Imrie and Peter Hall, in the preface to their book on inclusive design published in 2001, stated:

Physical barriers are compounded by social and attitudinal barriers which tend to regard disabled people as inferior and of little value ... Indeed disabled people often feel 'out of place' because of social and attitudinal markers of difference, ranging from people's indifference to them, to acts of hostility and even physical violence.

Not surprisingly, in combination with the physical configuration of the built environment, the socio-attitudinal nature of society is a powerful mechanism of social exclusion.[2]

David Morris, the Mayor of London's disability advisor, illustrated this attitude with a very powerful quote from a participant of the Disability Capital 2003 Survey:

The aggressive stuff is more easy to deal with somehow – it is just a shock when somebody crosses the street to spit in your face. When people dismiss you and exclude you and treat you like you are from another planet, that is when the veneer cracks and tears flood inside'.[3]

Many believe that this attitude has changed little in the last 15 years.

In my experience, the main impediment is staff attitudes – most are helpful and apologetic when a need is explained, but simply haven't thought about (or had training to think about) the practicalities of accessibility.'

Val Southon, Member of the City of London Access Group, June 2018[4]

Our attitude towards disabled people has a significant impact on how we design and create our buildings, places and spaces. We are gradually changing our attitude and our behaviour and it is having a lasting impact, but we still have much further to go. It took until the late 20th century before the Victorian approach to disabled people – confined to residential institutions – was challenged by disabled people themselves. Redefining what it means to be a disabled person and adopting the 'social model of disability' has liberated many disabled people and helped non-disabled people start to look at the barriers created in the built environment rather than at an individual's impairment. By embracing the social model of disability, we can all help to dismantle physical and organisational barriers and promote inclusion.

There have been incredible medical and technological advances in the last 30 years that have transformed and dramatically improved many lives, but the medical model of disability can and still does take away responsibility for demanding environmental and social change. This approach limits opportunities to live full and active lives. The social model of disability turns this on its head – it is the barriers in the environment and our attitude that results in disability, rather than the impairment itself. An accessible home or workplace will enable the individual to continue leading an active, fulfilled life, contributing to society and the economy.

The government aimed to create a lasting legacy for disabled people from the London 2012 Paralympic Games. One of three key aims was to 'influence the attitudes and perceptions of people to change the way they think about disabled people'. It was hoped that a successful Paralympic Games would 'raise awareness, help to challenge stereotypes and improve understanding'.[5]

London 2012 did increase the visibility and raise the profile of disabled people. Scope, in a survey of more than 1,000 disabled people just before the Rio 2016 Games, found that:

- 82 per cent of disabled people believed the Paralympics made disabled people more visible in wider society

- 78 per cent said the Paralympics improved attitudes

- 82 per cent said the Paralympics changed negative assumptions about disability.

But the statistics showed that disabled people continue to face negative attitudes, with little or no improvement across key areas of everyday life:

- Just 19 per cent of disabled people thought Britain was a better place to be disabled than in 2012.

- Less than a quarter thought that the accessibility of pubs, restaurants, clubs and shops had improved (23 per cent), and only 21 per cent thought transport had improved.

- Nearly 80 per cent of disabled people said there had been no change in the way people acted towards them.

Our attitude towards older people has similar consequences. An attitude of pity and sympathy – the 'charity model' – can be as limiting as the medical model, as can fear of disability and old age. An entrenched societal image of being young, fit and beautiful does not allow for difference. Trying to conform to some concept of 'being normal' can engender an attitude that does not consider or think about disability or even the natural ageing process, despite disability and impairment being a normal part of the human condition. Sophie Handler, in her book An Alternative Age-Friendly Handbook, refers to the way we tend to view ageing in terms of a 'demographic time bomb', using the language of 'apocalyptic demography', and suggests that 'looking beyond the physical fabric of the built environment and addressing relational and social dynamics can be seen as a new way of broadening out age inclusive urban practice'. However, if we don't get the physical right then the other elements can't easily follow – Sophie asks, 'If there is no accessible transport to get me from my home to my political meeting, how can I participate in local democracy?'[6]

Many misconceptions are reinforced by the use of the international wheelchair symbol. Helpful as it is, the symbol can result in disability being equated to wheelchair use only and a belief that accessible designs only benefit a small minority of people, so the millions of disabled people whose impairment is not visible remain ignored. This can lead to the assumption that by providing a ramp, a lift and a wheelchair-accessible toilet, the design will automatically qualify as accessible, missing a huge number of other design elements that enable easy access for everyone.

Lack of knowledge and understanding and an anxiety about not complying with legislation, regulations and technical standards can lead to unimaginative, medical-style designs which can make the scheme ugly and undesirable. Yet Chapter 4 has illustrated that inclusive access can be aesthetically pleasing and can win awards. Innovative and creative design can also be constricted by a fear of getting it wrong and worrying about the risk of being taken taking to court, leading to an approach to do the minimum required by legislation. Better understanding of the issues, better education and training and the direct involvement of disabled people can all help overcome these fears and result in more accessible and inclusive schemes.

Nothing about us without us

Local and strategic access groups

The benefits of students and designers working with disabled people who have lived experience of physical and environmental barriers and listening and learning from their experiences can be long term. Not only will the experience affect the particular scheme or project being considered, but by listening and understanding the issues, the designer will also take that knowledge into their next project.

The benefits of engaging with disabled people are clearly demonstrated by the success of the London Legacy Development Corporation (LLDC) Built Environment Access Panel (BEAP) and before it the Olympic Delivery Authority's BEAP. Both groups added significant value to the consultation process, with disabled people giving their views and suggestions for improvement prior to proposals being given planning permission (see Chapter 3). The groups benefited directly from their diverse membership – experienced professional access consultants alongside members of the community with lived experience of disability. Careful choice of membership, through a transparent and accessible selection process, greatly assisted the effectiveness and cohesiveness of the group.

Encouraging clients to appoint access consultants, and to involve disabled people from the start of the project through to completion, helps the professionals involved in delivering the scheme increase their inclusive design knowledge, skills and understanding. This can ensure the application of best practice standards and consistency of provision at all stages of development.

West Cheshire's Corporate Disability Access Forum (CDAF) demonstrates the impact an access group can have (Figure 6.1). Supported by Cheshire West and Chester Council, chaired by an elected councillor and with a regular active membership of disabled residents and representatives of local organisations of disabled people, CDAF helps to ensure that inclusive access is effectively considered by the designers of major schemes being proposed. The group meets regularly at an early stage in the design process – before detailed designs are fixed – and has ensured the provision of facilities such as the Changing Places WC and flexible seating arrangements in the Storyhouse theatre (see Chapter 4). CDAF's added value to the development process was recognised in 2015 when it won the Improved Mobility category in the government's Accessible Britain Challenge.[7]

Figure 6.1 **Members of West Cheshire's Corporate Disability Access Forum consider proposals for the development of the Northgate area of Chester, in 2015.**

Collective and co-production

Another opportunity to help embed the principles of inclusive design into a project is by co-production. As part of its drive to improve services and accessibility for all communities in the borough, Hammersmith and Fulham Council set up a Disabled People's Commission in 2016. The commission produced its final report in December 2017, called Nothing About Disabled People without Disabled People: Working Together to Transform Services in Hammersmith and Fulham. Regarding the definition of 'co-production', the report states: 'Co-production (working together) means local Disabled residents are working together with decision makers to actively identify, design and evaluate policy decisions and service delivery that affect our lives and remove the barriers we face'.[8]

One of the recommendations was that early consideration be given to co-production in specific policy areas, with the suggestion that plans to refurbish Hammersmith Town Hall and the surrounding area should be co-produced with disabled people to ensure that the plans were to the highest standard of inclusive design. The planning application for the Town Hall proposals is, at the time of writing, being considered by the council. The ambition to achieve an inclusive scheme is clearly articulated in the Design and Access Statement and the council's Disabled Residents Team (drawn from the Disabled People's Commission) has been closely involved in the development of the scheme, meeting regularly with designers. This has resulted in several areas where the scheme exceeds minimum standards. At the launch of the commission's report in June

2018, Mark Rintoul, architect for the scheme from Rogers Stirk Harbour + Partners, described this co-production work as 'an extremely beneficial collaboration'. He explained, 'The disabled residents' first-hand experience informed the design and allowed us to overcome some challenges. This level of community engagement is truly pioneering and one we fully endorse'.[9]

The Disabled Residents Team and the scheme's design team are now examining how well the co-production process embedded inclusive design principles into the project.

Working together meant that we [the Disabled Residents Team] were able to raise issues early so the design team had time to respond with robust solutions. We strongly recommend this way of working because not only can it save time and money, but disabled people were an integral part of creating a development that everyone can use.'

Member of the Hammersmith and Fulham Council Disabled Residents Team[10]

Is ignorance the enemy of inclusion?

The enemy of knowledge is not ignorance but the illusion of knowledge.'

Professor Stephen Hawking, at the opening ceremony of the London 2012 Paralympic Games[11]

A lack of inclusive design knowledge and skills can result in schemes that compromise inclusion. Learning directly from a variety of disabled people, as part of our basic training, will help us understand the impact our designs have on disabled and older people. However, the variety of the human condition is so vast that we often put this in the 'too difficult box' and carry on designing in our own image. A government initiative to encourage a more proactive approach to teaching and learning about access and inclusion was launched after the London 2012 Olympic and Paralympic Games.

The Built Environment Professional Education Project (BEPE)

> Entrenching inclusive design isn't just about changing attitudes but teaching through education and training. Designers, architects and engineers are too often not equipped, through courses and accreditation, to understand or take into account inclusivity and the needs of all end users. Teaching the next generation of engineers to consider the impact their work has on all societal groups should be a priority to ensure progress is not lost.'
>
> ICE Thinks: Inclusive Cities Discussion Paper[12]

On the advice of the Paralympic Legacy Advisory Group, set up as part of the UK government's 10-year Olympic and Paralympic Legacy Programme, the Built Environment Professional Education Project (BEPE) was launched in March 2014. The aim was to create a systematic change in how all built environment professionals are taught inclusive design.

Figure 6.2 **BEPE – the Built Environment Professional Education Project. This poster was created by the Office for Disability Issues in 2015 to promote the BEPE Project at conferences, seminars and exhibitions.**

The BEPE vision was that all newly qualified built environment professionals would complete their formal training and start their careers with the knowledge, skills and attitude to deliver accessible and inclusive buildings, places and spaces in all their projects (Figure 6.2).[13] This was to be achieved by embedding inclusive design as a core part of the required curriculum in the education of built environment professionals, with student assessments and Assessments of Professional Competence that would reflect this.

A system change was needed. It was not going to be enough just to add a few more occasional 'specialist' lectures, but the learning had to be integrated into existing programmes, so it became part of the normal way of teaching. Support was needed from those professional institutions that accredited and validated higher education courses, to ensure that those courses and those teaching the courses understood and implemented the necessary changes to make an impact.

Support was quickly forthcoming from all the major built environment professional institutions, including the RIBA, who stated:

> The Royal Institute of British Architects feels passionately that improving accessibility for disabled people forms a critical curricular element for all those involved in studying the built environment; we are proud therefore to support this wider industry drive. We will be working to develop criteria referencing inclusive design as part of our work with all recognised RIBA schools of architecture around the world to help lead this critical aspect of the design process. Building on the all-inclusive design ethos of the London 2012 Olympic and Paralympic Games, we will actively promote the design and management of future spaces with accessibility and good design at their core to the next generation of architects, engineers and planners.[14]

The project was given a major boost when the Quality Assurance Agency (QAA) reviewed several key built environment Subject Benchmark Statements. The QAA is the independent body that oversees standards in higher education in the UK. Its subject benchmark statements form part of the UK Quality Code for Higher Education and set out what graduates in a particular subject might reasonably be expected to know, do and understand at the end of their programme of study. The benchmark statements for Architectural Technology; Town and Country Planning; Landscape Architecture; Land, Construction, Real Estate and Surveying have all now been amended to include as a threshold standard the need for graduates to have knowledge and understanding of the principles and processes that deliver an inclusive environment.[15]

Time will tell whether the higher education sector embraces the standards and makes effective changes to its built environment programmes. Architecture and engineering are still to make changes to their accreditation criteria but have the opportunity to do this – the Architectural Registration Board as part of its current criteria review, and the Engineering Council as part of the next review of its UK Specification.

Support for change is increasingly evident. The need for improved education and training was recognised by the CIHT (Chartered Institution of Highways and Transportation) in its review of shared space, which concluded that there is a lack of skills in the engineering sector in relation to designing accessible environments, and a lack of understanding of the requirements of the Equality Act 2010. It recommended: 'Education and continuing professional development of those developing works in the public realm should specifically include the requirements around creating inclusive environments and accessibility. Professional institutions across the sector should take a lead in developing this approach'.[16]

The ICE Thinks event in March 2018 examined the role of the engineer in creating inclusive cities and asked, 'What is the scope and opportunity to place accessibility at the heart of decision-making on new and existing infrastructure assets?'[17] It raised a number of pertinent discussion points, including the need to educate engineers to think inclusively. Professor Lord Robert Muir, President of the Institution of Civil Engineers, said in his keynote speech, 'We need to inspire the next generation of engineers to think in new ways and have new approaches to creating truly inclusive cities'.[18]

This positive encouragement to the profession should have an impact and should encourage not just civil engineers, but all built environment professionals to improve their inclusive design knowledge and skills and crucially to implement the principles of inclusive design in all their projects.

The BEPE Project transferred to the Construction Industry Council (CIC) in 2016 to help with the transition from a government-driven project to an industry-owned and led project.

To assist the higher education sector to better embed inclusive design into its education programmes, the CIC published a briefing guide in 2017 and circulated it to the key higher education forums, including SCHOSA (Standing Conference of Heads of Schools of Architecture), the AAE (Association of Architectural Educators), the Planning Forum, ACED (the Association of Civil Engineering Departments) and CHOBE (Council of Heads of Built Environment).[19] The guide, Bringing Inclusive Design into Built Environment Education, illustrated the key issues in terms of improving knowledge, skills and understanding. The key messages for the education sector are as follows:

- All built environment professionals should finish their basic training with an understanding of the impact of their professional activities on the achievement of an inclusive environment.

- Training should include consideration of the impact of the built environment on the inclusion in society of disabled and older people.

- An inclusion-related cross-professional development programme should be established.

- The evidence base should be brought from research and practice into the realm of educators and policymakers.[20]

Inclusive design is now increasingly being added to institute CPD programmes and over time, as accredited higher education courses are re-validated by the institutions, inclusive design should become a more integrated feature of built environment courses, helping to embed the BEPE vision that:

- students learn the skills that make inclusive design second nature

- educators inspire students to acquire the knowledge, skills and confidence to make inclusion the norm not the exception

- professionals integrate the principles of inclusive design into all their projects.

New initiatives to improve skills and knowledge
The Design Council, whose vision is to make life better by design, enabling happier, healthier and safer lives for all, launched its Inclusive Environment Hub in 2014 – a collection of resources on inclusive design best practice guidance for built

environment professionals.[21] The hub includes links to a wide variety of advice and guidance documents on buildings and outdoor spaces in all phases of development, including planning, design and construction, through to the management of buildings and places. The Design Council has also launched an online Inclusive Environment CPD training programme, which should, by giving the strategic overview, help improve understanding of accessibility issues so that built environment professionals can deliver good inclusive design. It should also be a catalyst that prompts institutions to develop more specific CPD training for each built environment area of practice.

To stimulate interest from undergraduate and postgraduate design students, the Royal Society of Arts Student Design Awards competition, which has been running since 1924, has since 2016 included a brief to help inspire innovative and creative inclusive design projects. The competition challenges students and recent graduates to tackle pressing social, environmental and economic issues through design thinking. The first Inclusive Cities brief in 2016 encouraged the submission of designs, concepts, plans or strategies for a place or space in which to work, live, shop, do business or play. The 2018/19 brief, called Hidden Figures, asks:

'Design a way to break down the physical, organisational or attitudinal barriers that people with hidden disabilities or impairments can face in society, to enable them to live their lives to the full'.[22]

Supported by the Office for Disability Issues and sponsored by a different design company each year, the Student Design Awards encourage students to consider how to design inclusively.

DEC! (Design Engineer Construct!) is an accredited learning programme for secondary-school-age students, developed to create and inspire the next generation of built environment professionals.[23] It has also been encouraging students to learn about inclusive environments. In 2017 the Construction Industry Council and the Office for Disability Issues supported DEC! in its annual competition. The challenge – to 'design a home for everyone' – was open to all UK primary schools, secondary schools and first-year undergraduates. Students were asked to create the ideal inclusive house, using their creativity and ingenuity. By working with local disabled people, the winners produced excellent designs. The winners of the over-16s entry (see Figure 6.3) have been inspired to continue learning about buildings – one is now studying building surveying and one is studying building services engineering at college – two future

Figure 6.3 A 'House for All' was the winning design in the over-16s DEC! 'design a home for everyone' challenge in 2017.

built environment professionals who will start their careers with a better understanding of disability and inclusive design principles.[24]

Another initiative that will support the BEPE objective is the launch of a new teaching programme in the autumn of 2019 by the Global Disability Innovation Hub (GDIH) in east London (see Chapter 3). The GDIH has been working with University College London (UCL) to develop a new MSc course called Disability Design and Innovation. The aim is to enable students to apply innovative design thinking with a focus on disability. The course will be delivered by the GDIH and taught across Loughborough University London, London College of Fashion and UCL and will blend design engineering with global policy and the societal context of disability.

Topics covered in the MSc will include:

- future global technologies
- disability and development
- inclusive design and assistive technology
- research and making skills
- marketing and business.

By working across institutions, sectors and faculties, this innovative new course aims to teach students how to make a tangible difference to people's lives. Not only is this a great legacy from the London 2012 Olympic and Paralympic Games, it will also demonstrate new ways of teaching and learning about inclusive design.

Manchester School of Architecture, Westminster University and CASS School at London Metropolitan University have also been looking at innovative ways of bringing inclusive design training into the design studio. Jos Boys and Zoe Partington, co-founders of the DisOrdinary Spaces Architecture Project, have been exploring how disability and accessibility can be approached differently within architecture, interiors and related design practices. Working with disabled artists and educators, the project is creating a prototype of innovative and creative ways of teaching disability and inclusion. The website states:

> TheDisOrdinary Architecture Project believes that thinking differently about disability (and ability) can open up the design of our built surroundings to new forms of creativity and critique. Instead of treating disabled people as merely a 'technical' and 'legal' problem for architecture and urban design, we show how starting from disability – from the rich differences that biodiversity and neuro-divergence bring – is a powerful creative force for design. We bring together disabled artists with built environment practitioners, educators, students and others to explore how valuing different ways of being in the world can offer innovative alternatives to conventional and mundane 'access solutions'.[25]

Reading University responded to BEPE by setting up its Breaking down Barriers project in 2015, a cross-disciplinary project that is integrating inclusive design into the teaching and learning of a wide range of students, including students from the School of the Built Environment, the Henley Business

School, the School of Art and Communication Design and the Department of Real Estate and Planning. The aim is to enhance the student experience and employability by:

- developing a cross-disciplinary expert knowledge base
- prioritising experiential learning with a strong user focus
- engaging with real-world scenarios and external organisations.[26]

Students discuss and debate the principles of inclusive design, how designers can achieve inclusion in real-life projects, how design briefs often tend to create segregation and how designers can develop more inclusive solutions to briefs.

Encouraging clients to embrace an inclusive design approach

Inclusive Design is about maximising the market potential of your products by making sure the maximum number of people can use them.'

Simeon Keates and John Clarkson,
University of Cambridge[27]

Missing out on £249 billion

We are gradually starting to change our perceptions of disabled people, recognising that disabled people are consumers and customers, employees, business owners, company directors, entrepreneurs and political leaders. They are us. This shift in perceptions has been helped by the gradual increase (although still limited) of disabled people in the media. Presenters such as Ade Adepitan, Adam Hills and Alex Brooker now present mainstream not specialist 'disability' TV programmes. However, change is slow, and businesses continue to miss out on this largely untapped market.

Government statistics make the business case for inclusion absolutely clear. There are 13.3 million disabled people in the UK (one in five of us), with a total spending power of £249 billion (known as the 'purple pound').[28] Over 10 million people are affected by hearing loss, and 100 people begin losing their sight every day. If you ignore one disabled person, you ignore their friends, family and work colleagues, so it is in the interest of all businesses to ensure that their building, products and services are accessible to everyone – it makes sense financially. Disabled consumers themselves are rightly demanding the same consumer rights as non-disabled people. Increasing customer expectations should be an indication of the latent untapped market that many businesses are missing out on by not adapting their premises or changing the way they provide and deliver their service. Many product designers have now recognised and embraced inclusive design principles, but the construction industry has been much slower to address the issue.

> In a rapidly ageing world, it no longer makes commercial sense or social sense to design, develop or attempt to market products and services whose usability is unnecessarily challenging to people, whether they be young, old, able-bodied or less able.'
>
> Roger Coleman, Royal College of Art[29]

It is not just the purple pound that businesses are missing out on. We are all ageing healthier and wealthier and we want to continue consuming. The spending power of people over the age of 50 has been estimated at £320 billion in the UK (in 2012), with global spending power estimated to reach £15 trillion by 2020.[30] As the UK population continues to grow and age, the Third Age Economy will become more and more valuable – currently estimated to be 47 per cent of all consumer spending.[31] At the time of writing (2019), 18 per cent of the UK population was over the age of 65. By 2040 the number of people over the age of 75 is expected to double to 10 million, and by 2045 one in four of us will be 65 or over.[32] We want to continue leading independent and active lives and expect to be able to participate fully in life and contribute to society. If your product, service or building does not respond to the needs of older people you will miss out. It's not just about making places wheelchair accessible, important as this is, it is in all business interests to acquire a greater understanding of the needs of people living with dementia, autism and mental health issues and recognise their consumer value. More than 800,000 people in the UK are living with dementia, two thirds of whom live in the community in their own homes, not in care homes, and are therefore still out and about shopping, travelling and consuming.[33]

A good example is the hotel and travel industry. Older people spend billions of pounds each year on hotels and travel, but the industry loses billions by not targeting or responding to the needs of older consumers. Some efforts are being made to redress this balance, and some hotel chains have worked hard to make their accessible rooms less medical and more like all the other rooms in the hotel. Handrails and other equipment required by regulation are often used as an argument to provide only the minimum number of accessible rooms as their medical design may put off non-disabled customers. However, more hotels are now recognising that good inclusive design can result in rooms that look good, are wheelchair accessible and provide for a wider clientele. Walk-in showers with sensitively integrated handrails are a benefit to all of us, particularly for older people. Information on hotel websites detailing facilities available to disabled and older people has also improved – it is now so easy to upload photographs and video clips enabling customers to see exactly what facilities are offered – but this is still the exception rather than the rule.

The Dairy, Cottage in the Dales

One business is showing the way by developing a holiday home that is not just accessible but, by following the principles of inclusive design, is a delightful cottage for anyone. Cottage in the Dales, a luxury holiday cottage business in the Yorkshire Dales, realised after 11 successful years that 'a number of our more elderly guests were struggling to cope with the stairs that we have in both our existing properties – and that we were having to turn down new guests as a result of not having an accessible option'. The website explains, 'That got us thinking; how could we deliver the 5* experience that Cottage in the Dales prides itself on, but cater to a totally new "accessible" demographic?'[34]

By careful consideration of accessible and inclusive design, they converted the old dairy into a self-catering cottage that is not just accessible to disabled and older people, but also seamlessly blends the accessible features into a beautifully designed, good-looking cottage. The cupboards under the kitchen sink and under the cooker hob can be easily removed to provide legroom for a wheelchair user. The large walk-in shower in the bathroom has been designed so that the grab rails and the flip-down seat (supplied by Motionspot) can be quickly and easily removed when not needed (see Figures 6.4 and 6.5).

Following careful research and by adhering to Visit England's National Accessibility Scheme Standards, they provided facilities for guests with mobility, hearing and visual impairments[35] in an elegant and clever way, while creating a desirable, luxury cottage that is also well designed for non-disabled people. The video on their website and information on their accessibility page demonstrates what can be achieved by following inclusive design principles. The website states:

From the outset, our dream wasn't to just deliver an accessible property; we wanted to deliver our unique '5-star, Cottage in the Dales experience', but in an accessible way. Our vision was to bridge the gap between disabled and able-bodied, and deliver the same level of luxury experience, regardless of age or physical ability. Our research highlighted that due to a clinical feel, many disabled properties don't appeal to able-bodied guests, and in reverse many luxury properties were unsuitable for disabled guests. We wanted to change that.[36]

The business case is proven – Diane Howarth, the cottage owner, told me that fitting out The Dairy was no more expensive than fitting out The Byre across the courtyard, explaining that 'it is all in the planning'. The cottage is very popular – it was 96 per cent full in 2018, and by February 2019 it was 85 per cent booked for 2019 and bookings for 2020 were already at 22 per cent – demonstrating its success and its popularity with returning guests (split 50/50 between disabled and non-disabled customers). However, Diane and her husband Andrew are not complacent – they plan to meet with Accessible Derbyshire/ Access for All UK to get advice on what they can do to make the cottage more welcoming for people with autism – so widening their clientele even further. Not only is the cottage physically accessible, but Diane and Andrew provide a high level of customer service too – they have spent time researching the accessibility of local amenities and visitor attractions in the area in order to provide information on their accessibility to their disabled guests.

Recognised nationally for tourism and building, The Dairy won the Visit England Awards for Excellence: Bronze Award for Inclusive Tourism 2018 and the LABC (Local Authority Building Control) Building Excellence Award for Best Inclusive Building in England and Wales 2018.[37]

Figure 6.4 **The Dairy, Yorkshire: the accessible features in the bathroom (grab rails and a shower seat) can be installed or removed as required.**

Figure 6.5 **The Dairy, Yorkshire: in the kitchen, the cupboards under the sink and under the hob can be removed to provide space for a wheelchair user to manoeuvre easily and there are pull-out shelves under the oven.**

> 'Inclusive design is not just about taking into account disability, but about putting safety and ease of use for all people first. Ensuring people of all backgrounds, cultures, ages and incomes can use infrastructure independently, have choice and where possible, without the need for help, through convenient and welcoming design.'
>
> ICE Thinks: Inclusive Cities Discussion Paper[38]

The impact of lottery funding

Many owners and developers of arts, cultural and heritage buildings have been influenced by the need to improve accessibility and inclusivity in order to receive lottery funding. Since the National Lottery was launched in 1994 and the National Lottery Arts Capital Access Guidelines and Checklists have been used by distributors of lottery funding, access for disabled people has been part of the funding application process, resulting in a significant shift in approach and attitude.

The Arts Council's funding procedures have made a substantial impact on how owners of theatres, museums, art galleries and music venues respond to the need to make their buildings accessible. The Arts Council's access policy, checklist and action plan provides a guide to increasing participation in the arts by disabled people as artists as well as audience members and employees.[39] Applicants for lottery funding must demonstrate how their building is to be made accessible for disabled people. Expert access consultants are asked to assess the funding applications and assist applicants to meet and go beyond minimum standards. Schemes only receive funding if the proposal meets the access policy guidelines.

> 'In the early days many organisations had never heard of access audits or access consultants, let alone the concept of inclusive design. It was our job to provide applicants with the tools to help them make the right decisions from a more enlightened position, to ask the right questions of their design teams, and to enable the organisations to continue to learn and develop the skills to manage their new or improved venues. The ultimate goal was to facilitate a change in the culture of the organisation to become inclusive and welcoming to all.'
>
> Jayne Earnscliffe, Access Consultant and Arts Council England assessor, monitor and advisor[40]

Exemplar schemes include not only specialist organisations such as Graeae Theatre Company and its award-winning Bradbury Studios but also an extensive list of mainstream art galleries, music venues, museums and theatres, which have all significantly improved their accessibility and inclusivity over the years as a direct result of the Arts Council's access policy. The Arts Council's guidelines are currently being updated to reflect the growing expectations of disabled performers as well as an increasingly diverse audience and the need to further mainstream inclusive access.

Similarly, the Heritage Lottery Fund (HLF) has had a significant impact on the accessibility of historic buildings and landscapes. Grant applicants are asked to address the HLF inclusion guidance, which asks applicants to understand the barriers people face and what changes could be made to their project to help people feel welcome. This can include using a registered access consultant to undertake an access audit to assess any physical barriers that may need to be removed or overcome by use of reasonable adjustments. Funding for capital works and activities is dependent on achieving the HFL inclusion outcome that 'a wider range of people will have engaged with heritage'.[41]

Missing out on talent

There needs to be a change in disabled people being seen as people that can add value, not just people who sit at home doing nothing. If they are then that's probably because society is creating barriers that means that they can't.'

Equality and Human Rights Commission[42]

If a building or service is not accessible, businesses will lose valuable customers, but businesses are also missing out on talent. The disability employment gap (the gap between the employment rate for disabled people and the employment rate overall) is 32 per cent in the UK and many disabled people are able and want to work.[43] There is a skills shortage across many industries, so this pool of talent should not be ignored.

The intention of the government's Access to Work scheme and initiatives such as Disability Confident is to make it easier for businesses to understand and meet the needs of disabled employees, but these initiatives do not appear to make any substantial difference to the number of employers willing to employ and retain disabled people. The narrative sometimes seen in the press of 'benefit scroungers' fuels false assumptions that disabled people can't work or don't want to work, but this could not be further from the truth. Challenging these attitudes and helping clients to see the business benefits of inclusion can and does result in a change of mind-set.

Inclusion champions

One of the challenges designers sometimes face is encouraging their clients to go beyond the very minimum regulatory standards. One solution is to continually improve the legislation and regulations to raise minimum standards and, as we have seen, there is still scope to improve both planning policy and building regulations. However, if leaders in the construction industry – those with the power and authority to demand inclusion in their schemes – champion inclusion from the outset, designers, planners, surveyors and project managers are all more likely to be able to achieve high standards of accessible and inclusive design in their projects. To encourage those who own and pay for development to become inclusion champions and take responsibility for achieving an inclusive development process, the Construction Industry Council published an Essential Principles Guide for Clients, Developers and Contractors: Creating an Accessible and Inclusive Environment.

Encouraging clients to adopt and implement these principles will help to achieve change and may lead to a construction industry we can all be proud of.

Essential Principles for Clients, Developers and Contractors

- **Champion** and commit to achieving an accessible and inclusive environment in your **Strategic Vision**.

- In your **Project Brief** set out what tools, mechanisms and processes you will use to implement an **Inclusive Development Process**.

- Structure your **Budget** from the outset for implementing your **Inclusive Design Strategy**.

- Make addressing inclusive design principles a requirement of your **Procurement Process** and in your development agreements.

- **Use Access and Inclusive Design Expertise** throughout the process and engage and consult effectively with diverse users.

- **Monitor and Appraise** the outcomes of your approach and use lessons learnt to enhance future projects.[44]

Looking forward to an inclusive future

Much continues to be written about the social aspects of disability discrimination and how society considers equalities issues, whether in relation to gender, race, sexuality, religion, faith, age or disability (from books by Michael Oliver and Colin Barnes to more recent texts from Jos Boys and Aimi Hamraie).[45] Our inability to comprehensibly address accessible and inclusive design is absolutely constrained by this societal attitude and the resulting institutionalised disability discrimination that is still endemic. Why is it still OK to segregate disabled people at an entrance into a public building, treating them differently to those who can use a revolving door (Figure 6.6). We would think it wholly unacceptable to segregate in this way on grounds of race or gender.

Figure 6.6 **You have to ring for assistance or find the push plate before you can open this 'accessible' entrance door.**

Aimi Hamraie, in her book Building Access, suggests an intersectionality approach – looking at the similarities between gender, race, sexuality and disability discrimination may help us to understand why discrimination persists and why social justice for disabled people, women, transgender and black and minority ethnic people still evades us. This may help to effect positive change.[46] A new concept – 'inclusive equality' – was adopted in April 2018 by the UN Committee on the Rights of Persons with Disabilities by General Comment No 6, as a way of 'combatting stigma, stereotyping, prejudice and violence'; recognising 'the dignity of human beings and their intersectionality'; and 'the full recognition of humanity through inclusion in society'. It re-states the responsibilities of signatories to the Convention (which includes the UK government) and recognises that, despite the introduction of anti-discrimination legislation and actions to promote equality and tackle discrimination, there continues to be a need to recognise that:

 laws and regulatory frameworks often remain imperfect and incomplete or ineffective or reflect an inadequate understanding of the human rights model of disability. Many national laws and policies perpetuate the exclusion and isolation of and discrimination and violence against persons with disabilities. They often lack a recognition of multiple and intersectional discrimination or discrimination by association; fail to acknowledge that the denial of reasonable accommodation constitutes discrimination; and lack effective mechanisms of legal redress and reparation.'[47]

A change in societal values, attitudes and behaviours will certainly help to create a more responsive, dynamic, innovative and ultimately a more inclusive way to design, build and manage our built environment. We can all become inclusion champions.

'Inclusivity is not a buzzword; it has a real impact on real lives … We need to challenge ourselves, our industry, government and the wider public to change how we do things in order to benefit everyone in society …

Social exclusion can be minimised by inclusive design.'

ICE Thinks: Inclusive Cities Discussion Paper [48]

Are you an inclusive designer?

To reinforce the message that inclusive design is a professional obligation and that the goal of achieving inclusion should be integrated into an individual's professional code of conduct, the Construction Industry Council published 'Essential Principles for Built Environment Professionals: Creating an Accessible and Inclusive Environment'. Six principles were chosen to help guide, support and motivate individual professionals when making decisions for clients. The professional institutions supporting the BEPE Project endorsed these principles and agreed to promote them to their members.

Essential Principles for Built Environment Professionals

1. Contribute to building an inclusive society now and in the future.
2. Apply professional and responsible judgement and take a leadership role.
3. Apply and integrate the principles of inclusive design from the outset of a project.
4. Do more than just comply with legislation and codes.
5. Seek multiple views to solve accessibility and inclusivity challenges.
6. Acquire the skills, knowledge, understanding and confidence to make inclusion the norm not the exception.[49]

We can ask government to lead by example and require inclusion in all government-funded projects and improve legislation and regulations, but to create an inclusive environment we must all take responsibility – both professionally and personally – to challenge discrimination and promote and implement inclusive practices. It is in all our best interests to keep on pursuing the ambition of an accessible and inclusive environment, not just for disabled people, for people with long-term health conditions or for older people, but for ourselves, our families and our friends – inclusive design is for all of us, and we must work harder to achieve it.

There are opportunities to create better legislation and better regulations, provide more effective tools, address inclusion from the outset of projects, embed inclusive design requirements into procurement and tendering processes, improve planning and building control processes, and implement best practice technical standards and robust enforcement processes throughout all construction stages, along with better inclusive design education and training for all built environment professionals. Collectively this may eventually help to change attitudes and behaviours in the construction industry. But at the end of the day, the responsibility lies with each and every one of us. So my final recommendations (see box, overleaf) are aimed at helping all of us to adopt and implement the practice of inclusive design.

Implement the principles of inclusive design from the outset of all projects:

- Place people at the heart of the design process
- Offer choice not a single solution
- Provide for flexibility in use
- Create places that are convenient and enjoyable for everyone
- Acknowledge diversity and difference

The Practice of Inclusive Design

Challenge disability discrimination and promote equality:

- Recognise the impact prejudiced attitudes have and help change behaviours
- Empower diverse users through co-production
- Make access inclusive not special or separate
- Embrace the business case and recognise the value of inclusive buildings
- Help develop profession specific learning tools

Implement an Inclusive Development Process:

- Champion inclusion in your Strategic Vision

- Integrate your Inclusive Design Strategy into your Project Brief

- Structure your budget to address inclusive design from the outset

- Make inclusion integral to your procurement process

- Monitor and appraise outcomes in use and management

Aim to achieve the highest standards of access and inclusion in all projects:

- Go beyond minimum legislation

- Know, use and implement best practice standards

- Use policy, regulations and technical advice effectively

- Learn from best practice in existing and historic buildings

Use Access expertise throughout the project

- Recognise that inclusion is a key part of sustainable development

Conclusion

Utopia, or just good design?

We have seen how a Roman temple, a walled city, a mediaeval crypt and even a Wren cathedral have been made accessible. We have seen how a beach hut, a holiday cottage, leisure and arts centres, through to major sporting venues, can be designed to be inclusive. We have seen a shift from the single family bathroom with one WC in a home, to the addition of a downstairs WC, to en-suite bathrooms with walk-in showers becoming the norm. We have seen a shift from stepped, to ramped and stepped entrances, and on to early consideration of site topography to create level entrances. We have seen a shift from separate, often locked, 'accessible' entrance doors beside a revolving door, to automatic sliding doors that everyone can use – although this shift is still not happening fast enough! We are gradually seeing building legibility integrated from the outset of design, not left to sign designers at the end of the fitout, and we are seeing an increasing use of colour and contrast, and a choice of audible and tactile information, to help show building users around a space.

By putting people at the heart of designs, and by understanding how a variety of different people perceive, use and experience buildings and spaces, designers are creating not just accessible buildings – places that we can enter and use, but where we may need assistance, or be directed to separate or segregated facilities – but are increasingly creating inclusive buildings – places where we can all have the same enjoyable, safe and comfortable experience, regardless of our personal circumstances.

We've seen how inclusion makes sense economically, how an accessible building costs no more than an inaccessible one, and how good design can help businesses thrive.

This is all worth celebrating, but we also know that many new homes are still being built today without walk-in showers, and without the space needed to easily move around and be comfortable as our needs change. We continue to see separate facilities, or no facilities at all, built into new and refurbished buildings, and fashions in street design that make some people feel vulnerable. We have still not learnt how to make all buildings safe and comfortable for people with mental ill health, learning disabilities, dementia or autism, despite increasing numbers of schemes demonstrating how to mainstream 'design for the mind'. Neither must we leave behind the importance of individual requirements: exclusive design that is person-centred and ensures facilities are designed to suit an individual's circumstances. Providing choice, recognising diversity and making space for difference as a matter of human dignity are fundamental elements of inclusion.[1] Above all, we cannot be complacent. We must be vigilant and continue to strive towards making inclusive design a normal part of any development process.

An inclusive environment is not a utopian dream. It can and is being achieved, albeit often on an ad hoc basis. Creativity, imagination and determination are needed to drive effective change beyond the individual building level, to the neighbourhood level and to a city-wide scale. This can be achieved, and examples are emerging, but it has taken over half a century, from when access issues were first considered by designers up to the second decade of the 21st century, to start making any real impact.

More ethical behaviour is being introduced into architectural, engineering and other built environment professions, and this is to be celebrated. If we demand from our clients, our professional bodies, our local and national politicians, from our friends and neighbours and from ourselves, we can all become inclusion champions. If the government leads by example with its infrastructure and development programme and the private sector (both commercial and residential) follows, and if each and every architect, designer, and built environment professional learns the skills, uses their inclusive design knowledge, engages with a diverse range of users, and embraces the principles of inclusive design – then we can create an inclusive environment in our lifetime.

Inclusive Design is Good Design

Appendices

Appendix 1

Stratford City Consultative Access Group:
Protocol for accessible presentations

Guidance for speakers at SCCAG meetings

The SCCAG is a diverse group of disabled people with a range of access needs. The group is committed to making sure that everyone is able to take part fully in all meetings. These guidelines are to help you play your part in making our meetings fully accessible. If you have any questions about our meetings, please contact the Chair.

Preparations for meeting:

If sending papers to the group, please refer to your guidance on Access to Written Material.

At meetings:

- Please introduce yourself and explain what your role is and why you have come to the meeting.

- Explain what you are going to talk about and what you would like the SCCAG members to do (comment, make recommendations, etc).

- Avoid jargon, acronyms and explain any unusual terms. Use very plain English. Keep statements simple and sentences short – no more than one or two thoughts per sentence.

- If you are talking about policy issues, explain what they mean in practice. Do not assume that everyone in your audience knows how the construction industry works.

- Speak steadily – not too fast. Remember to pause frequently to give the sign language interpreters time to operate.

- If using PowerPoint, or similar, read out what is on the screen. If there are diagrams, explain them verbally – do not assume everyone can see or understand them.

- Check with the group that they are all following what you are saying. You can either do this by asking directly, or by asking for reactions to what you have said. If the responses do not quite match what you have asked, the reason is probably that you have not been completely understood.

- At the end of the presentation, summarise the main points.
- Keep your presentation as brief as possible.

Dealing with questions from the group

- Expect members to ask questions during your presentation; recognise that asking some members to wait until the end may mean they cannot participate (try to be flexible).
- If you do not understand someone's speech, it is infinitely better to ask them to repeat what they have said rather than to speculate. Do not interrupt or finish the sentences of people with speech impairments. Give people time to make their point.
- Always speak directly to Deaf or disabled people, i.e. not to their personal assistant, facilitator or to the sign language interpreters.
- Be prepared to answer questions.

When an audience includes blind or partially sighted people:

- on-screen narrative should always be read in full
- on-screen pictures, drawings and graphics should be described*
- on-screen site plans should be portrayed using points of the compass to illustrate the relative position of significant features*
- whenever possible use tactile plan/maps to enhance your description.

(*all subsequent commentary should relate to the key reference points established during the initial description/portrayal)

When an audience includes Deaf or hearing-impaired people:

- Initially it is essential to ensure that the assistive hearing system (AHS), e.g. induction loop or infra-red system, is functioning effectively at all times; it is equally important to conduct all dialogue, without exception, with the assistance of the AHS. (It is worth noting that induction loops can only be used by people with a hearing aid or assistive listening device. Do not assume that all people with a hearing loss will be able to make use of these systems. It is important to ask in advance what support they would prefer.)

- In the course of larger meetings, at which roving microphones are not available, it is necessary to reiterate questions from your audience before providing an answer.

- In order to enable the full participation of those who lip-read it is vital to remain highly visible but not in front of bright lights or an intense glare (please recognise also that the habit of covering one's lower face with your hands can effectively camouflage any meaningful conversation with lip-readers; as equally can the sporting of an unkempt, bushy moustache!).

- If you are using sign language interpreters, it is useful to send them meeting notes and/or PowerPoint presentations in advance so that they can prepare, especially when more technical words are used.

- Make certain that sign language interpreters also have access to highly visible location at all times – during 'black-out' periods for video/film showings, ensure that interpreters remain in a maintained spot-light.

- Allow time for interpreters to translate: giving them a glossary in advance may be helpful, as some terms may be unfamiliar to participants in their first language.

- Always wait for the interpreter to translate what has been said before responding.

- Some deaf people prefer to use a palantypist (if their first language is English rather than BSL). Palantypists need time to set up their equipment in advance of the meeting and so this should be built into the timings.

Presenting technical issues

Consultation on access issues frequently requires participants with widely different skills and perspectives [to find] a common language and understanding of the factors and process involved. It is often necessary for highly trained professionals to make presentations in lay terms and to clarify the meaning of architectural/technical drawings in everyday language, particularly if the combined experiences of all interests concerned are to be of benefit to the overall objective.

It is the case that architectural drawings are often not readily understood by lay people, disabled or otherwise, and the translation of scaled-down, 2 dimensional drawings into recognisable 3-dimensional images can often prove to be a slow process. It is therefore essential that, when using any form of technical drawings, presenters ensure that their audience is able to translate and fully understand all the material/information offered.

There are simple solutions to this problem:

- Initially take the time to clarify what it is that the drawings concerned are seeking to illustrate.

- Where circumstances permit, offer training on how to read drawings in advance of an actual presentation. Avoid technical jargon.

- Select the simplest of plans available; if necessary use a succession of similar drawings which become progressively more detailed.

- Make sufficient copies of the drawings used to enable the whole audience to easily follow the presentation.

- Clarify the thinking and logic behind the overall orientation of buildings and site features.

- Explain the limitations of the site/building, i.e. its listed status, the topography, its history and intended purpose.

- Seek to illustrate a clear sense of perspective and how space will be used, e.g. including scale furniture or vehicles will help show the size of rooms and widths of thoroughfares.

- Tactile plans will help blind and partially sighted people read the plans.

- Talk the audience through the plans, e.g. which areas will change, what standards will be used, which features are the potential barriers.

- Take the audience on an imaginary journey through the site or building. A sequential journey: describe each area and its proposed features – highlight the envisaged layout, routes and important access provisions, e.g. where the lifts are located in relation to the reception desk and why.

- a model of the building – a model of the site or building as it is and as it is proposed can be extremely helpful. A scale model, rather than a 2-dimensional plan, makes it much easier for most people to imagine how a site or building will look; it also tends to illustrate more understandably how a development will function and perform.

- Where the technology allows, use 3D computer simulation of a journey through a building or site – but don't forget to make the information accessible to visually impaired people.

In the course of any presentation it is the responsibility of presenters to accommodate all the needs of their audience, particularly those with sensory impairments, e.g. generally there should always be adequate lighting levels and, without fail, an appropriate assistive hearing facility.

Terminology

It should be noted that terms such 'the disabled' and 'the blind' are not welcome as they endorse the unacceptable notion that disabled people are all of some homogenous characteristic rather than being as diverse and individual as any other random group of people.

It is similarly unwelcome to misrepresent inclusive facilities as 'disabled', e.g. accessible toilets are not 'disabled' – such references tend only to perpetuate outdated 'special needs' thinking.

Appendix 2

Stratford City Consultative Access Group: Protocol for written material

- All documents to be in 16 point Ariel or similar sans serif typeface.

- Documents will be accepted from other departments and organisations only if they are in minimum 14 point, Ariel or similar. 16 point is preferred (electronically circulated papers can use smaller fonts).

- All documents in black print on light paper, preferably white.

- All documents should be left aligned (not justified to page width).

- Avoid reversed out text, do not use italics (to highlight issues use bold or underline).

- Tables, charts etc. must be in minimum 14 point Ariel. Where possible avoid tables and charts as they are more difficult to convert into other formats and cannot be read by some audio translators.

- Avoid jargon.

- Any acronyms or initials should be referenced or spelt-out in full.

- Documents of more than 6 pages should be circulated to members only if a one- to two-page easy-read summary is also provided.

- The chair reserves the right to refuse any document that is considered not to be accessible to all group members.

- All business papers for circulation to members should reach the chair at least two weeks before the meeting.

- All technical documents should be provided by the Developer at least 10 days prior to the meeting.

- SCCAG will not accept significant written documents tabled at meetings as these may not be accessible to some members.

- Speakers wishing to provide written information for members to take away after meetings should ensure that these are set out in a relevant accessible format. Please check in advance with the Chair.

- Appropriate tactile, Braille and audio alternatives must be made available when necessary.

Appendix 3

Stratford City Consultative Access Group: Lessons learnt and transferability to other projects[1]

All of the following lessons can be transferred to other major, multi-phase development projects:

Ensure consultative access group framework in place

Ensuring that the appropriate framework is in place, whether this is via a Section 106 Agreement or agreed terms of reference and protocols, was essential. Clearly establishing the funding and the operative provisions for SCCAG, including the collaborative nature of its membership, has been the cornerstone of its successful operation.

Early engagement (RIBA Stage B [now Stage 1])

Early engagement between the developers, their design team and the review panel has made a significant difference to the quality of the agreed detailed designs. It has also helped to enable a collaborative approach to design development.

Representative and competent panel

Ensuring that the composition of the panel is both representative and competent. In this case, the careful composition of the membership and the leadership of the Chairman meant that SCCAG gave clear and robust advice to design teams and to the Local Planning Authority. This provided certainty for developers, reduced risk and assisted with the timely and efficient management of planning applications. It also enabled a shared dialogue with design teams on minimum standards and the aspirations to go beyond these.

Establish protocol

The establishment of a protocol for presentations to the review panel ensured a clarity and consistency of response and comments on detailed designs. Innovative techniques, such as the preparation of the tactile plans, assisted not just the group but also broader public consultation work to the benefit of the project as a whole.

Abbreviations

AAE	Association of Architectural Educators
AAP	Access Adaptations Programme
ACE	Access Committee for England
ACED	Association of Civil Engineering Departments
ANSI	American National Standards Institute
APC	Assessment of Professional Competence
ARB	Architects Registration Board
ATP	Accessible Transport Panel
BB	Building Bulletin
BEAP	Built Environment Access Panel
BEPE	Built Environment Professional Education Project
BRE	Building Research Establishment
BSI	British Standards Institution
BSL	British Sign Language
CABE	Commission for Architecture and the Built Environment
CAE	Centre for Accessible Environments
CCS	Considerate Contractor Scheme
CCSS	Considerate Contractor Streetworks Scheme
CHOBE	Council of Heads of Built Environment
CIAT	Chartered Institute of Architectural Technologists
CIC	Construction Industry Council
CIHT	Chartered Institution of Highways and Transportation
CIOB	Chartered Institute of Building
CPD	Continuing Professional Development
CSDPA	Chronically Sick and Disabled Persons Act

DCLG	Department for Communities and Local Government
DCMS	Department for Culture, Media and Sport
DDA	Disability Discrimination Act
DfT	Department for Transport
DPTAC	Disabled Persons Transport Advisory Committee
DRC	Disability Rights Commission
DWP	Department for Work and Pensions
EHRC	Equality and Human Rights Commission
FLA	Football Licensing Authority
GDIH	Global Disability Innovation Hub
GLA	Greater London Authority
GOE	Government Olympic Executive
HE	Historic England
ICE	Institution of Civil Engineers
LABC	Local Authority Building Control
LAF	London Access Forum
LLDC	London Legacy Development Corporation
LOCOG	London Organising Committee of the Olympic and Paralympic Games
MHCLG	Ministry of Housing, Communities and Local Government
NPPF	National Planning Policy Framework

ODA	Olympic Delivery Authority
ODI	Office for Disability Issues
PAS	Publicly Accessible Standard
QAA	Quality Assurance Agency
RADAR	Royal Association of Disability and Rehabilitation
RCA	Royal College of Arts
RIBA	Royal Institute of British Architects
RICS	Royal Institution of Chartered Surveyors
RNIB	Royal National Institute of Blind People
RSA	Royal Society of Arts
RTPI	Royal Town Planning Institute
SBS	Subject Benchmark Statement
SCCAG	Stratford City Consultative Access Group
SCHOSA	Standing Conference of Heads of Schools of Architecture
TfL	Transport for London
UCL	University College London
UN	United Nations
UPIAS	Union of the Physically Impaired Against Segregation
WDA	Wandsworth Disablement Association

Bibliography

Boys, J, *Doing Disability Differently*, Routledge, London, 2014

Boys, J (ed), *Disability, Space, Architecture: A Reader*, Routledge, Oxford, 2017

British Standard Code of Practice BS 8300:2018-1 and BS 8300:2018-2, *Design of an Accessible and Inclusive Built Environment*, British Standards Institution, London, 2018, https://shop.bsigroup.com/ProductDetail?pid=000000000030335835 (accessed 13 February 2019)

CABE, *The Principles of Inclusive Design (They Include You)*, Commission for Architecture and the Built Environment, London, 2006, https://www.designcouncil.org.uk/sites/default/files/asset/document/the-principles-of-inclusive-design.pdf (accessed 13 February 2019)

Centre for Ageing Better, *Room to Improve: The Role of Home Adaptations in Improving Later Life*, Centre for Ageing Better, London, 2017, https://www.ageing-better.org.uk/publications/room-improve-role-home-adaptations-improving-later-life (accessed 13 February 2019)

CIHT, *Creating Better Streets: Inclusive and Accessible Spaces – An Industry Review of Shared Space*, Chartered Institution of Highways and Transportation, London, 2018, https://www.ciht.org.uk/news/ciht-launches-creating-better-streets-an-industry-review-of-shared-space (accessed 13 February 2019)

Cook, G and Fleck, J, *Teaching and Learning Briefing Guide: Bringing Inclusive Design into Built Environment Education*, Construction Industry Council, 2017, http://cic.org.uk/projects/project.php?s=teaching-and-learning-briefing-guide (accessed 13 February 2019)

Department for Transport, *The Inclusive Transport Strategy: Achieving Equal Access for Disabled People*, HM Government, London, 2018, https://www.gov.uk/government/publications/inclusive-transport-strategy/the-inclusive-transport-strategy-achieving-equal-access-for-disabled-people (accessed 13 February 2019)

Fleck, J, 'Inclusive design – A lasting Paralympic legacy? Embedding inclusive design knowledge and skills into architectural education',

Charrette 2(1), autumn 2015, https://architecturaleducators.wordpress.com/aae-journal/charrette-21 (accessed 26 March 2019)

Goldsmith, S, *Designing for the Disabled: The New Paradigm*, Architectural Press, Oxford, 1997

Grant, A, *Designing for Accessibility*, Centre for Accessible Environments and RIBA Publishing, London, 2012

Grant, A, *Access Audit Handbook*, Centre for Accessible Environments, London, 2013

Hamraie, A, *Building Access: Universal Design and the Politics of Disability*, University of Minnesota Press, Minneapolis, 2017

House of Commons Women and Equalities Committee, *Building for Equality: Disability and the Built Environment*, HC 631, 2017, https://www.parliament.uk/business/committees/committees-a-z/commons-select/women-and-equalities-committee/inquiries/parliament-2015/disability-and-the-built-environment-16-17 (accessed 13 February 2019)

ICE, *ICE Thinks: Inclusive Cities Discussion Paper, What is the City but the People? The Role of the Engineer in Creating Inclusive Cities*, Institution of Civil Engineers, London, 2018, https://www.ice.org.uk/getattachment/news-and-insight/ice-thinks/growing-cities-and-building-resilience/what-is-the-city-but-the-people/Inclusive-Cities-discussion-paper_lowest-res-for-web.pdf.aspx (accessed 18 March 2019)

Imrie, R and Hall, P, *Inclusive Design: Designing and Developing Accessible Environments*, Spon Press, London, 2001

Keates, S and Clarkson, J, *Countering Design Exclusion: An Introduction to Inclusive Design*, Springer, London, 2004

Live Tourism with Arkenford, *Games Changer? An Evaluation of London as an Accessible Visitor Destination*, Greater London Authority, London, 2013, https://www.london.gov.uk/sites/default/files/games_changer_report.pdf

London Legacy Development Corporation, *Inclusive Design Strategy*, LLDC, London, 2012, https://www.queenelizabetholympicpark.co.uk/-/media/qeop/files/public/inclusivedesignstrategymarch2013.ashx?la=en (accessed 13 February 2019)

London Legacy Development Corporation, *Inclusive Design Standards*, LLDC, London, 2013, https://www.queenelizabetholympicpark.co.uk/-/media/ qeop/files/public/inclusivedesignstandardsmarch2013.ashx?la=en (accessed 13 February 2019)

Mayor of London, The London Plan Supplementary Planning Guidance, *Accessible London: Achieving an Inclusive Environment*, Greater London Authority, London, 2004, https://webarchive.nationalarchives.gov.uk/ tna/20141208074702/http://www.london.gov.uk/sites/default/files/archives/ spg_accessible_london.pdf (accessed 25 March 2019)

Mayor of London, *Shaping Neighbourhoods, Accessible London: Achieving an Inclusive Environment*, Supplementary Planning Guidance, London Plan 2011 Implementation Framework, Greater London Authority, London, 2014, https://www.london.gov.uk/sites/default/files/shaping_neighbourhoods_ accessible_london_spg_2014.pdf (accessed 25 March 2019)

Ministry of Housing, Communities and Local Government, *National Planning Policy Framework*, HM Government, London, 2018, https://www.gov. uk/government/collections/revised-national-planning-policy-framework (accessed 13 February 2019)

Office for Disability Issues and Mayor of London, *Built Environment Professional Education Project: Report of Progress March 2016*, Department for Work and Pensions, HM Government, London, 2016, https://www.gov.uk/ government/publications/built-environment-professional-education-project- progress-report (accessed 13 February 2019)

Olympic Delivery Authority, *Inclusive Design Strategy*, ODA, London, 2008, https://webarchive.nationalarchives.gov.uk/20110802172830 http:/www.london2012.com/documents/oda-equality-and-diversity/inclusive- design-strategy-september-2008.pdf (accessed 13 February 2019)

Olympic Delivery Authority, *Inclusive Design Standards*, ODA, London, 2011, https://webarchive.nationalarchives.gov.uk/20120824144426/ http:/learninglegacy.london2012.com/documents/pdfs/equality-inclusion- employment-and-skills/62-inclusive-design-standards-eies.pdf (accessed 13 February 2019)

Porteus, J and Park, J, *Age-Friendly Housing: Future Design for Older People*, RIBA Publishing, London, 2018

Further information

Professional bodies

The key built environment professional bodies, including the RIBA, RTPI, ICE, RICS and CIHT, supported the government's Built Environment Professional Education Project (BEPE) and agreed that every built environment professional should have 'the knowledge, skills and attitude to deliver accessible and inclusive buildings, places and spaces.'[1] They also agreed to promote among their members the Construction Industry Council's 'Essential Principles for Built Environment Professionals.'[2] The institutes should therefore be embedding inclusive design into the education and training of all their members and actively promoting a more inclusive environment. If your own professional institution is not running any CPD events or training programmes, or providing information and resources on inclusive design specific to your profession, then do please lobby them to do so and remind them of their commitment to this issue.

Local authority access officers

Local authority access officers can be a great source of local advice at planning policy and planning application stage, with building regulation applications, Blue Badge parking provision and other local access issues. They can help interpret inclusive design planning policies and have often produced supplementary planning guidance (for example the Greater London Authority, Islington Council, Leeds Council, Manchester Council and many more).[3]

They often work directly with a local access group of disabled residents, so can help with setting up a project-specific access forum or with consultation and engagement events.

Unfortunately, the number of local authorities employing specialist access officers has considerably reduced following reductions in local government funding and the introduction of austerity measures, but where they are still employed, they are a great resource. The Access Association can help identify which local authorities employ specialist access/inclusive design staff.[4]

National Register of Access Consultants (NRAC)

NRAC is an independent UK-wide accreditation service whose members provide independent access and inclusive design advice. Consultancy and auditor services include: inclusive design advisory services for projects, access audits of existing environments, policy and procedural advice, assistance with Heritage Lottery and other funding, and access and inclusive design training.[5]

Design Council

The Design Council launched its Inclusive Design Hub in 2014 and its online CPD training programme in 2019.[6] The Hub is a collection of resources on inclusive design and best practice and includes links to a wide variety of advice and guidance documents on buildings and outdoor spaces in all phases of development, including planning, design and construction, through to the management of buildings and places. If you are aware of any documents missing from the Hub, the Design Council would be happy to hear from you.

Centre for Accessible Environments (CAE)

The Centre for Accessible Environments has been helping to deliver inclusive environments through its consultancy training, advice and guidance services to developers, designers, construction organisations, managers and occupiers of buildings since 1969. Now the consultancy trading arm of Habinteg Housing Association, it continues to provide a range of inclusive design advice services, undertakes research projects and produces useful guidance publications.[7]

Organisations of disabled people

Organisations of disabled people have the expertise and experience to clearly and accurately articulate the barriers many people face every day. Spending a few minutes reading the online news feed of organisations such as Disability Rights UK – an organisation of disabled people 'leading change and working for equal participation for all' – provides an instant picture of current issues, frustrations and campaigns.[8]

Many organisations run campaigns on specific access issues. For example, the personal stories that Habinteg Housing Association gathered as part of its 'For Accessible Homes' campaign demonstrates the impact inaccessible homes are having on the lives of disabled people and helps us to better understand the benefits of accessible housing.[9] Leonard Cheshire's campaign on the hidden housing crisis and its more recent survey on access to pubs and bars highlight the difficulties many disabled people still face.[10]

Notes and references

Acknowledgments

1   Mayor of London press release, '*2012 Games raising bar for embedding accessibility into sporting venues and city infrastructure*', Greater London Authority, 30 August 2012, https://www.london.gov.uk/press-releases-4813 (accessed 11 February 2019); see also.
Baroness Grey-Thompson DBE, *Inclusive Design at Queen Elizabeth Olympic Park*, London Legacy Development Corporation video, http://www.queenelizabetholympicpark.co.uk/our-story/transforming-east-london/accessibility (accessed 11 February 2019).

Introduction

1   https://www.designcouncil.org.uk/what-we-do/built-environment/inclusive-environments (accessed April 2018).
2   British Standard Code of Practice BS 8300:2018, *Design of an Accessible and Inclusive Built Environment,* British Standards Institution, London, 2018.

Chapter 1

1   House of Commons Women and Equalities Committee, *Building for Equality: Disability and the Built Environment*, HC 631, 2017, https://www.parliament.uk/business/committees/committees-a-z/commons-select/women-and-equalities-committee/inquiries/parliament-2015/disability-and-the-built-environment-16-17 (accessed 13 February 2019).
2   British Standard Code of Practice CP96:1967, *Access for the Disabled to Buildings,* British Standards Institution, London, 1967.
3   ASA A117.1-1961, *American Standard Specifications for Making Buildings and Facilities Accessible to, and Usable by, the Physically Handicapped*, American Standards Association, New York, 1961.
4   Selwyn Goldsmith, *Designing for the Disabled,* RIBA Publications, London, first edition, 1963.
5   Selwyn Goldsmith, *Designing for the Disabled: The New Paradigm*, Architectural Press, Oxford, 1997.
6   Tim Nugent, quoted in Selwyn Goldsmith, *Designing for the Disabled: The New Paradigm*, p 16.
7   Changing Places Consortium, http://www.changing-places.org (accessed 11 February 2019).

8   https://www.gov.uk/government/news/ministers-act-to-increase-changing-places-toilets-for-severely-disabled-people (accessed 11 February 2019).

9   Housing Development Directorate, *Occasional Paper 2/74 Mobility Housing*, HMSO, London, 1974.

10 Housing Development Directorate, *Occasional Paper 2/75 Wheelchair Housing*, HMSO, London, 1975.

11 The Building Regulations 2010, *Access To and Use of Buildings, Approved Document M, Volume 1: Dwellings,* HM Government, Newcastle Upon Tyne, 2015.

12 https://disability-studies.leeds.ac.uk/wp-content/uploads/sites/40/library/Barnes-implementing-the-social-model-chapter-2.pdf (accessed 11 February 2019).

13 https://disability-studies.leeds.ac.uk/library/author/oliver.mike (accessed 11 February 2019).

14 British Standard Code of Practice BS 5810:1979, *Access for the Disabled to Buildings,* British Standards Institution, London, 1979.

15 Silver Jubilee Committee on Improving Access for Disabled People, *Can Disabled People Go Where You Go?* Department of Health and Social Security, London, 1979.

16 Borough Planner's Service, *Public Consultation: Access to Buildings and Spaces for People with Disabilities, Wandsworth Borough Plan, Planning Policy and Design Guidelines*, Wandsworth Borough Council, London, 1988.

17 Access Committee for England and the Royal Town Planning Institute, *Access Policies for Local Plans: An Access Policy Package*, The Royal Town Planning Institute, London, 1993.

18 Department of the Environment, *Planning Policy Guidance 1: General Policies and Principles (PPG1),* HM Government, London, 1992.

19 Letter from Tony McNulty MP to the author (who was at the time access officer at the GLA), dated 24 March 2003.

20 Department for Communities and Local Government Circular 01/2006, *Guidance on Changes to the Development Control System*, HM Government, London, 2006.

21 Commission for Architecture and the Built Environment, *Design and Access Statements: How to Write, Read and Use Them*, CABE, London, 2006.

22 Office of the Deputy Prime Minister, *Planning Policy Statement 1: Delivering Sustainable Development*, HM Government, London, 2005.

23 Office of the Deputy Prime Minister, *Planning and Access for Disabled People: A Good Practice Guide*, HM Government, London, March 2003,

https://assets.publishing.service.gov.uk/government/uploads/system/ uploads/attachment_data/file/7776/156681.pdf (accessed 11 February 2019).

24 Mayor of London, *The London Plan: Spatial Development Strategy for Greater London,* Greater London Authority, London, 2004, https://www. london.gov.uk/what-we-do/planning/london-plan/past-versions-and-alterations-london-plan/london-plan-2004 (accessed 20 March 2019), pp 178–9.

25 Mayor of London, *The London Plan Supplementary Planning Guidance, Accessible London: Achieving an Inclusive Environment*, Greater London Authority, London, 2004, https://www.london.gov.uk/sites/default/files/gla_ migrate_files_destination/archives/spg_accessible_london.pdf (accessed 11 February 2019).

26 Mayor of London, *The London Plan: Spatial Development Strategy for Greater London, Draft for Public Consultation,* Greater London Authority, 2017, https://www.london.gov.uk/sites/default/files/new_london_plan_ december_2017.pdf (accessed 20 March 2019), p 13.

27 Ibid, p 106.

28 https://www.london.gov.uk/what-we-do/planning/london-plan/new-london-plan/download-draft-london-plan-0 (accessed 11 February 2019).

29 Ibid.

30 Patrick Jenkin, Secretary of State for the Environment, quoted in Selwyn Goldsmith, *Designing for the Disabled: The New Paradigm*, p 90.

31 Frank Duffy, quoted in Selwyn Goldsmith, *Designing for the Disabled: The New Paradigm*, p 92.

32 Center for Universal Design, *The Principles of Universal Design*, North Carolina State University, Raleigh, 1997.

33 Ibid.

34 Inclusive Design Group Engineering Design Centre, Department of Engineering, University of Cambridge, *Inclusive Design Toolkit*, http:// www.inclusivedesigntoolkit.com (accessed 11 February 2019).

35 CABE, *The Principles of Inclusive Design (They Include You),* Commission for Architecture and the Built Environment, London, 2006, https://www.designcouncil.org.uk/sites/default/files/asset/document/the-principles-of-inclusive-design.pdf (accessed 11 February 2019).

36 British Standard Code of Practice BS 8300:2018, *Design of an Accessible and Inclusive Built Environment*, British Standards Institution, London, 2018.

37 https://www.architecture.com/knowledge-and-resources/knowledge-landing-page/bsi-concentrates-on-design-for-the-mind-guidelines (accessed 11 February 2019).

38 https://disability-studies.leeds.ac.uk/wp-content/uploads/sites/40/library/ disability-rights-task-force-drtf.pdf (accessed 14 March 2019); see also Department for Education and Employment, *Towards Inclusion – Civil Rights for Disabled People: Government Response to the Disability Rights Task Force*, HM Government, London, March 2001, http://webarchive. nationalarchives.gov.uk/+/http:/www.dft.gov.uk/transportforyou/access/ dda2005/pubs/drtf/towardsinclusion (accessed 11 February 2019).

39 Alison Grant, *Access Audit Handbook,* Centre for Accessible Environments, London, 2013 (originally published in 2005). Alison Grant, *Designing for Accessibility,* Centre for Accessible Environments and RIBA Publishing, London, 2012 (originally published in 2004).

40 http://www.nrac.org.uk (accessed 11 February 2019).

Chapter 2

1 Department of Transport Disability Unit Circular DU1/86, *Textured Footway Surfaces at Pedestrian Crossings*, HM Government, London, 1986; see also Department of Transport Disability Unit DU 1/91, *The Use of Dropped Kerbs and Tactile Surfaces at Pedestrian Crossing Points*, HM Government, London, 1992.

2 *Reducing Mobility Handicaps: Towards a Barrier-Free Environment*, The Institution of Highways and Transportation, 1991.

3 City of London Considerate Contractor Scheme, https://www. cityoflondon.gov.uk/services/transport-and-streets/roads-highways-and-pavements/Pages/Considerate-Contractor-and-Considerate-Contractor-Streetworks-Scheme.aspx (accessed 11 February 2019).

4 *Designing an Accessible City*, Corporation of London, 1998.

5 Note to the author from Val Southon, member of the City of London Access Group, June 2018.

6 https://tfl.gov.uk/transport-accessibility (accessed 11 February 2019).

7 Note to the author from Sarah Morgan, chair of the City of London Access Group, June 2018.

8 http://data.parliament.uk/writtenevidence/committeeevidence.svc/ evidencedocument/women-and-equalities-committee/disability-and-the-built-environment/written/40737.html (accessed 11 February 2019).

9 The City of London Transport Strategy Draft for consultation, *City Streets, Transport for a Changing Square Mile,* November 2018, City of London Corporation, https://www.cityoflondon.gov.uk/services/transport-and-streets/Pages/transport-strategy.aspx (accessed 11 February 2019).

Chapter 3

1   Mayor of London press release, '*2012 Games* raising bar for embedding accessibility into sporting venues and city inf*rastructure*', Greater London Authority, 30 August 2012, https://www.london.gov.uk/press-releases-4813 (accessed 11 February 2019).
Baroness Grey-Thompson DBE, *Inclusive Design at Queen Elizabeth Olympic Park*, London Legacy Development Corporation video, http://www.queenelizabetholympicpark.co.uk/our-story/transforming-east-london/accessibility (accessed 11 February 2019).

2   Stephen Frost, *The Inclusion Imperative: How Real Inclusion Creates Better Business and Builds Better Societies*, Kogan Page Ltd, London, 2014, p 1.

3   Olympic Delivery Authority, *Inclusive Design Strategy*, ODA, London, 2008, https://webarchive.nationalarchives.gov.uk/20130403013222/http://learninglegacy.independent.gov.uk/themes/masterplanning-and-townplanning/case-studies.php (accessed 2.6.19)

4   http://learninglegacy.independent.gov.uk/documents/pdfs/sustainability/22-sustainable-development-strategy-sust.pdf (accessed 11 February 2019).

5   Mayor of London, The London Plan Supplementary Planning Guidance, *Accessible London: Achieving an Inclusive Environment*, Greater London Authority, London, 2004, https://www.london.gov.uk/sites/default/files/gla_migrate_files_destination/archives/spg_accessible_london.pdf (accessed 11 February 2019).

6   Olympic Delivery Authority Learning Legacy, *Stratford City Consultative Access Group: Inclusive Access and Design,* 2011, https://webarchive.nationalarchives.gov.uk/20130403014534/http://learninglegacy.independent.gov.uk/publications/stratford-city-consultative-access-group-inclusive-acces.php (accessed 11 February 2019).

7   Ibid.

8   Olympic Delivery Authority, *Inclusive Design Strategy*, 2008 page 8.

9   Olympic Delivery Authority, *Inclusive Design Strategy*, Appendix 1, p 19, https://webarchive.nationalarchives.gov.uk/20110802172830/http://www.london2012.com/documents/oda-equality-and-diversity/inclusive-design-strategy-september-2008.pdf (accessed 17 February 2019).

10 Olympic Delivery Authority, *Inclusive Design Standards*, Appendix 1, p 83, https://webarchive.nationalarchives.gov.uk/20120824144426/http:/learninglegacy.london2012.com/documents/pdfs/equality-inclusion-employment-and-skills/62-inclusive-design-standards-eies.pdf (accessed 17 February 2019).

11 https://www.disabilityinnovation.com (accessed 11 February 2019).

12 Live Tourism with Arkenford, *Is London Ready to Welcome Disabled Visitors?*, London Development Agency, London, 2010, http://webarchive.nationalarchives.gov.uk/20100505155725/http://www.lda.gov.uk/server.php?show=ConWebDoc.3596 (accessed 11 February 2019).

13 'Deaf' with a capital 'D' refers to people who identify as culturally Deaf and whose first language is British Sign Language.

14 See endnote 1.

15 Live Tourism with Arkenford, *Games Changer? An Evaluation of London as an Accessible Visitor Destination,* Greater London Authority, London, 2013, https://www.london.gov.uk/sites/default/files/games_changer_report.pdf (accessed 11 February 2019).

16 Emma Christie, *Projections of Demand and Supply for Accessible Hotel Rooms in London, Working Paper 90,* GLA Economics, November 2017, https://www.london.gov.uk/sites/default/files/accessible-hotel-rooms-wp90.pdf page 14 (accessed 11 February 2019).

17 London Development Agency, *Inclusive Design Toolkit*, LDA, 2007, https://webarchive.nationalarchives.gov.uk/20120326142548/http://www.lda.gov.uk/publications-and-media/publications/inclusive-design-toolkit.aspx (accessed 13 March 2019).

18 Mayor of London, *Shaping Neighbourhoods, Accessible London: Achieving an Inclusive Environment*, Supplementary Planning Guidance, London Plan 2011 Implementation Framework, Greater London Authority, London, 2014, https://www.london.gov.uk/sites/default/files/shaping_neighbourhoods_accessible_london_spg_2014.pdf (accessed 13 March 2019), p 101–3.

19 British Standard Code of Practice BS 8300:2018, *Design of an Accessible and Inclusive Built Environment*, British Standards Institution, London, 2018.

Chapter 4

1 https://www.thesill.org.uk/visit/accessibility (accessed 12 February 2019).
2 https://www.euansguide.com/venues/the-sill-bardon-mill-7343/reviews/
   excellent-facilities-5775 (accessed 8 March 2019). Euan's Guide is
   an online resource where disabled people review, share and discover
   accessible places to go.
3 https://www.euansguide.com/venues/yha-the-sill-at-hadrians-wall-
   hexham-8844/reviews/excellent-new-hostel-with-accessible-family-
   rooms-8150 (accessed 12 February 2019).
4 https://www.civictrustawards.org.uk/the-award/selwyn-goldsmith-award
   (accessed 8 March 2019)
   The Selwyn Goldsmith Award recognises universal design that works 'for
   all people, irrespective of age, ethnicity, gender or ability'. The judges
   look for schemes that have created 'an environment or building that is
   responsive, flexible, welcoming, easy to use and occupy; allowing all to
   use with dignity and equality'. To be considered for an award, the project
   should have gone 'beyond the building regulations, as a minimum using
   best practice guidance, putting people at the heart of the project and
   showing exemplar design'.
5 https://www.sportengland.org/media/3624/portway-lifestyle-centre-2014.
   pdf (accessed 12 February 2019).
6 https://www.gallaudet.edu/campus-design-and-planning/deafspace
   (accessed 12 February 2019).
7 Information from https://www.gallaudet.edu/campus-design-and-planning/
   deafspace (accessed 12 February 2019), reproduced here with kind
   permission from Hansel Bauman, Galludets University.
8 https://www.architecture.com/awards-and-competitions-landing-page/
   awards/riba-regional-awards/riba-north-west-award-winners/2017/
   liverpool-philharmonic (accessed 12 February 2019).
9 http://www.attitudeiseverything.org.uk/news/liverpool-philharmonic-
   awarded-gold-on-the-charter (accessed 12 February 2019).
10 Ibid.
11 https://www.civictrustawards.org.uk/winners/storyhouse-chester
   (accessed 12 February 2019).
12 https://www.euansguide.com/venues/storyhouse-chester-8263/reviews/
   their-house-is-everyones-house-7271 (accessed 12 March 2019).
13 https://homemcr.org/visit/facilities-and-access/access-information
   (accessed 12 February 2019).

14 Penton's report is cited in *'Where architecture aims at eternity: The perpetual challenge of access at St Paul's'*, Access by Design, Issue 122, Spring 2010, Centre for Accessible Environments; see also John Penton also authored *Widening the Eye of the Needle: Access to Church Buildings for People with Disabilities,* Church House Publishing, London, 2008.

15 *Equal Access Project St Paul's Cathedral, Design and Access Statement*, Caroe Architecture, July 2017, http://www.planning2. cityoflondon.gov.uk/online-applications/applicationDetails. do?activeTab=summary&keyVal=OU0KO8FHLG600 (accessed 12 February 2019). (The planning application drawings can be viewed on the City of London website using reference 17/00790/FULL.)

16 https://www.civictrustawards.org.uk/winners/national-army-museum (accessed 12 February 2019). https://www.civictrustawards.org.uk/the-award/selwyn-goldsmith-award (accessed 12 March 2019).

17 https://www.londonmithraeum.com/visit/#accessibility (accessed 12 February 2019).

18 Live Tourism with Arkenford, *Games Changer? An Evaluation of London as an Accessible Visitor Destination,* Greater London Authority, London, 2013, https://www.london.gov.uk/sites/default/files/games_changer_ report.pdf (accessed 12 February 2019).

19 http://www.attitudeiseverything.org.uk/the-charter-of-best-practice (accessed 12 February 2019).

20 https://www.youtube.com/watch?v=6RddBQ8ObLU (accessed 12 February 2019).

21 https://www.theo2.co.uk/visit-us/accessibility (accessed 12 February 2019).

22 https://www.bournemouth.gov.uk/AttractionsLeisure/ BeachesandWaterfront/AccessibleSeafront.aspx (accessed 12 February 2019).

23 British Standard Code of Practice, BS 8300-1:2018 *Design of an Accessible and Inclusive Built Environment. External Environment,* British Standards Institution, London, 2018.

Chapter 5

1 http://data.parliament.uk/writtenevidence/committeeevidence.svc/
   evidencedocument/women-and-equalities-committee/disability-and-the-
   built-environment/written/40816.html (accessed 11 February 2019).
2 Policy BN.5: Requiring Inclusive Design, *Legacy Corporation Local Plan
   (July 2015)*, London Legacy Development Corporation, 2015, http://
   www.queenelizabetholympicpark.co.uk/-/media/lldc/local-plan/local-
   plan-review-2017/7-section-6-creating-a-high-quality-built-and-natural-
   environment.ashx?la=en (accessed 11 February 2019).
3 Ministry of Housing, Communities and Local Government, *National
   Planning Policy Framework,* HM Government, London, 2018, https://
   www.gov.uk/government/publications/national-planning-policy-
   framework--2 (accessed 11 February 2019).
4 Ibid, footnote 46, p 39.
5 Mayor of London, *The London Plan: Spatial Development Strategy for
   Greater London*, Greater London Authority, London, 2011, see Policy 7.2
   An Inclusive Environment, p 212.
6 Dame Judith Hackitt, *Building a Safer Future: Independent Review of
   Building Regulations and Fire* Safety, Final Report, HM Government,
   London, 2018, https://assets.publishing.service.gov.uk/government/
   uploads/system/uploads/attachment_data/file/707785/Building_a_Safer_
   Future_-_web.pdf (accessed 11 February 2019).
7 Ibid, p 8.
8 CIC, *Essential Principles for Clients, Developers and Contractors:
   Creating an Accessible and Inclusive Environment*, Construction Industry
   Council, London, 2018, http://cic.org.uk/projects/project.php?s=essential-
   principles-guide-for-clients-developers-and-contractors (accessed 11
   February 2019).
9 CIC, *Essential Principles for Clients, Developers and Contractors*, p 8.
10 https://www.gov.uk/government/publications/national-infrastructure-and-
   construction-pipeline-2017#history (accessed 11 February 2019).
11 Infrastructure and Projects Authority, *Transforming Infrastructure
   Performance*, Cabinet Office/HM Treasury, HM Government, London, 2017.
12 https://www.islington.gov.uk/birth-death-marriage-and-citizenship/
   marriage-and-civil-partnerships/how-to-license-a-venue/city-of-london-
   venues-advice-and-forms (accessed 19 February 2019).
13 https://www.gov.scot/publications/licensing-scotland-act-2005-guidance-
   completing-disabled-access-facilities-statement (accessed 11 February
   2019).

14 https://www.un.org/sustainabledevelopment/blog/2016/06/disability-is-not-inability-says-ban-urging-equal-rights-for-all-to-achieve-global-goals (accessed 11 February 2019).

15 https://www.breeam.com/discover/technical-standards/communities (accessed 11 February 2019).

16 *BREEAM Communities Technical Manual* 2012, BRE, 2012, http://www.breeam.com/communitiesmanual/#03_step03/04_se_15_inclusive_design.htm%3FTocPath%3DStep%25203%2520Designing%2520the%-2520details%7C-3 (accessed 11 February 2019).

17 https://www.breeam.com/discover/technical-standards/newconstruction (accessed 11 February 2019).
https://www.breeam.com/NC2018/#04_management/man01_a.htm%3FTocPath%3D4.0%2520Management%7C_____1 (accessed 11 February 2019).

18 https://content.historicengland.org.uk/images-books/publications/easy-access-historic-landscapes/heag011-easy-access-to-historic-landscapes.pdf (accessed 11 February 2019).

19 https://historicengland.org.uk/advice/hpg/compliantworks/equalityofaccess (accessed 11 February 2019).

20 https://www.theguardian.com/cities/2017/sep/20/chester-europes-most-accessible-city_(accessed 11 February 2019).

21 Centre for Ageing Better, *Room to Improve: The Role of Home Adaptations in Improving Later Life*, Centre for Ageing Better, London, 2017,
https://www.ageing-better.org.uk/sites/default/files/2017-12/Room%20to%20improve.%20The%20role%20of%20home%20adaptations%20in%20improving%20later%20life.pdf (accessed 11 February 2019).

22 Department for Communities and Local Government, English Housing Survey, HM Government, London, 2016, https://www.gov.uk/government/collections/english-housing-survey (accessed 22 March 2019).

23 http://www.lifetimehomes.org.uk (accessed 11 February 2019).

24 British Standard Code of Practice BS 9266:2013, *Design of Accessible and Adaptable General Needs Housing*, British Standards Institution, London, 2013.

25 https://www.equalityhumanrights.com/en/housing-and-disabled-people-britain%E2%80%99s-hidden-crisis (accessed 11 February 2019).

26 *No Place Like Home*, Leonard Cheshire Disability, Home Truths Campaign, https://www.leonardcheshire.org/get-involved/campaigns/previous-campaigns (accessed 11 February 2019).

27 https://www.equalityhumanrights.com/sites/default/files/housing-and-disabled-people-britains-hidden-crisis-main-report_0.pdf (accessed 22 March 2019), pp 6–10.

28 https://www.parliament.uk/business/committees/committees-a-z/commons-select/communities-and-local-government-committee/news-parliament-2017/housing-for-older-people-report-17-19 (accessed 11 February 2019).

29 https://www.ageing-better.org.uk/publications/role-home-adaptations-improving-later-life (accessed 11 February 2019).

30 Jeremy Porteus and Julia Park, *Age-Friendly Housing: Future Design for Older People*, RIBA Publishing, London, 2018.

31 Mayor of London, *The London Plan: Spatial Development Strategy for Greater London, Draft for Public Consultation,* Greater London Authority, London, 2017, see Policy T2, pp 403–5.

32 https://www.rca.ac.uk/research-innovation/helen-hamlyn-centre/research-projects/2011-projects/out-order-problem-public-toilets-older-people (accessed 11 February 2019).

33 https://www.cityoflondon.gov.uk/services/transport-and-streets/clean-streets/Pages/Community-Toilet-Scheme-(CTS).aspx (accessed 11 February 2019).

34 *Table of Minor Suggested Changes to the Draft New London Plan*, Greater London Authority, August 2018, https://www.london.gov.uk/what-we-do/planning/london-plan/new-london-plan/download-draft-london-plan-0 (accessed 11 February 2019).

35 CIHT, *Creating Better Streets: Inclusive and Accessible Spaces – An Industry Review of Shared Space,* Chartered Institution of Highways and Transportation, London, 2018.

36 https://www.ciht.org.uk/news/ciht-launches-creating-better-streets-an-industry-review-of-shared-space (accessed 13 February 2019).

37 Department for Transport, *The Inclusive Transport Strategy: Achieving Equal Access for Disabled People*, HM Government, London, 2018, https://www.gov.uk/government/publications/inclusive-transport-strategy/the-inclusive-transport-strategy-achieving-equal-access-for-disabled-people (accessed 11 February 2019).

38 https://www.parliament.uk/business/committees/committees-a-z/commons-select/women-and-equalities-committee/news-parliament-2017/enforcing-the-equality-act-launch-17-19 (accessed 11 February 2019).

Chapter 6

1   Mary Beard, *Women and Power: A Manifesto*, Profile Books, London, 2017.
2   Rob Imrie and Peter Hall, *Inclusive Design: Designing and Developing Accessible Environments*, Spon Press, London, 2001, p ix.
3   Mayor of London, *Another Planet? Disabled and Deaf Londoners and Discrimination: The Interim Results of the Disability Capital 2003 Survey*, Greater London Authority, London, 2003.
4   Note to the author from Val Southon, a member of the City of London Access Group, June 2018.
5   Department for Culture, Media and Sport and Office for Disability Issues, *London 2012: A Legacy for Disabled People – Setting New Standards, Changing Perceptions*, London, 2010, https://webarchive.nationalarchives.gov.uk/+/http:/www.culture.gov.uk/images/publications/GOE_London_2012_Disability_Legacy.pdf (accessed 26 March 2019).
6   Sophie Handler, *An Alternative Age-Friendly Handbook,* University of Manchester Library/UK Urban Ageing Consortium/MICRA, Manchester, 2014.
7   https://www.gov.uk/government/news/groups-honoured-for-life-changing-work-at-house-of-commons-ceremony (accessed 11 February 2019).
8   https://www.lbhf.gov.uk/councillors-and-democracy/resident-led-commissions/disabled-people-s-commission (accessed 11 February 2019).
9   https://www.lbhf.gov.uk/articles/news/2018/06/disabled-residents-help-hammersmith-fulham-council-revolutionise-how-it-makes-decisions (accessed 18 March 2019).
10 Ibid.
11 https://assets.publishing.service.gov.uk/government/uploads/system/uploads/attachment_data/file/556955/black-and-white-built-environment-professional-education-project-report-of-progress.pdf (accessed 18 March 2019), p 17.
12 *ICE Thinks: Inclusive Cities Discussion Paper, What is the City but the People? The Role of the Engineer in Creating Inclusive Cities*, Institution of Civil Engineers, London, 2018, https://www.ice.org.uk/getattachment/news-and-insight/ice-thinks/growing-cities-and-building-resilience/what-is-the-city-but-the-people/Inclusive-Cities-discussion-paper_lowest-res-for-web.pdf.aspx (accessed 18 March 2019), p 12.

13 https://www.gov.uk/government/publications/built-environment-professional-education-project-updates/read-what-supporters-say-about-the-bepe-project (accessed 11 February 2019).

14 Office for Disability Issues and Mayor of London, *Built Environment Professional Education Project: Report of Progress March 2016*, Department for Work and Pensions, HM Government, London, 2016, https://assets.publishing.service.gov.uk/government/uploads/system/uploads/attachment_data/file/556955/black-and-white-built-environment-professional-education-project-report-of-progress.pdf (accessed 18 March 2019), p 34.

15 See, for example, Quality Assurance Agency for Higher Education, *Subject Benchmark Statement, Land, Construction, Real Estate and Surveying*, QAA, Gloucester, October 2016, https://www.qaa.ac.uk/docs/qaa/subject-benchmark-statements/sbs-land-construction-real-estate-and-surveying-16.pdf?sfvrsn=4998f781_10 (accessed 18 March 2019).

16 CIHT, *Creating Better Streets: Inclusive and Accessible Places – Reviewing Shared Space*, Chartered Institution of Highways and Transportation, London, 2018, https://www.ciht.org.uk/media/4463/ciht_shared_streets_a4_v6_all_combined_1.pdf (accessed 18 March 2019), p 24.

17 *ICE Thinks: Inclusive Cities Discussion Paper,* p 13.

18 https://www.ice.org.uk/news-and-insight/ice-thinks/growing-cities-and-building-resilience/what-is-the-city-but-the-people (accessed 26 March 2019).

19 Geoff Cook and Julie Fleck, *Teaching and Learning Briefing Guide: Bringing Inclusive Design into Built Environment Education*, Construction Industry Council, London, 2017, http://cic.org.uk/projects/project.php?s=teaching-and-learning-briefing-guide (accessed 11 February 2019).

20 Ibid, p 25.

21 https://www.designcouncil.org.uk/what-we-do/built-environment/inclusive-environments (accessed 11 February 2019).

22 https://www.thersa.org/globalassets/images/sda-18/sda-19/sda1819_hiddenfigures-.pdf (accessed 18 March 2019).

23 https://designengineerconstruct.com (accessed 11 February 2019).

24 https://designengineerconstruct.com/competitions/home-everyone-design-challenge (accessed 11 February 2019).

25 http://disordinaryarchitecture.com/wp (accessed 26 March 2019).

26 http://blogs.reading.ac.uk/breaking-down-barriers/2015/07 (accessed 18 March 2019).

27 Simeon Keates and John Clarkson, *Countering Design Exclusion: An Introduction to Inclusive Design*, Springer, London, 2004, Preface.

28 https://www.gov.uk/government/statistics/family-resources-survey-financial-year-201516 (accessed 11 February 2019). https://assets.publishing.service.gov.uk/government/uploads/system/uploads/attachment_data/file/572187/spending-power-of-disabled-people-and-their-families-2014-15.pdf (accessed 11 February 2019).

29 Roger Coleman, Royal College of Art, in Simeon Keates and John Clarkson *Countering Design Exclusion*, Foreword.

30 Cebr, *Consumer Spending Key Trends among the Over 50s, A report for Saga*, February 2014, http://www.cpa.org.uk/cpa-lga-evidence/Saga/Saga(2014)-Consumer_spending_key_trends_among_the_over_50s.pdf (accessed 18 March 2019).

31 Office for National Statistics, *Family Spending in the UK*, HM Government, 2017.

32 https://www.gov.uk/government/publications/inclusive-transport-strategy/the-inclusive-transport-strategy-achieving-equal-access-for-disabled-people (accessed 19 March 2019).

33 https://www.scie.org.uk/dementia/about (accessed 11 February 2019).

34 www.cottageinthedales.co.uk/holiday-cottages/39/Accessibility (accessed 19 March 2019).

35 https://www.visitenglandassessmentservices.com/our-schemes/national-accessiblescheme/

36 www.cottageinthedales.co.uk/holiday-cottages/39/Accessibility (accessed 19 March 2019).

37 https://www.labc.co.uk/news/case-study-best-inclusive-design-winner-dairy-cottage-dales?language_content_entity=en (accessed 17 February 2019).

38 *ICE Thinks: Inclusive Cities Discussion Paper,* p 12.

39 Arts Council England, *Disability Access: A Good Practice Guide for the Arts*, 2003, https://webarchive.nationalarchives.gov.uk/20160204124115/http://www.artscouncil.org.uk/advice-and-guidance/browse-advice-and-guidance/disability-access-a-good-practice-guide-for-the-arts (accessed 19 March 2019).

40 http://earnscliffe.associates/how-we-can-help (accessed 11 February 2019).

41 https://www.heritagefund.org.uk/publications/inclusion-guidance (accessed 26 March 2019).

42 https://www.equalityhumanrights.com/en/housing-and-disabled-people-britain%E2%80%99s-hidden-crisis (accessed 11 February 2019).

43 https://publications.parliament.uk/pa/cm201617/cmselect/cmworpen/56/5602.htm (accessed 11 February 2019).

44 CIC, *Essential Principles for Clients, Developers and Contractors: Creating an Accessible and Inclusive Environment*, Construction Industry Council, London, 2018, http://cic.org.uk/news/article.php?s=2018-09-11-essential-principles-guide-for-clients-developers-and-contractors (accessed 11 February 2019), p 3.

45 Michael Oliver, *The Politics of Disablement: A Sociological Approach*, Macmillan, London 1990; see also Colin Barnes, *Disabled People in Britain and Discrimination: A Case for Anti-Discrimination Legislation*, C Hurst & Co Publishers Ltd, London, 1991; see also Jos Boys (ed), *Disability, Space, Architecture: A Reader*, Routledge, Oxford, 2017.

46 Hamraie, A, *Building Access: Universal Design and the Politics of Disability,* University of Minnesota Press, Minneapolis, 2017.

47 United Nations Convention on the Rights of Persons with Disabilities, Committee on the Rights of Persons with Disabilities, *General Comment No 6 (2018) on Equality and Non-Discrimination,* https://tbinternet.ohchr.org/_layouts/treatybodyexternal/Download.aspx?symbolno=CRPD/C/GC/6&Lang=en (accessed 14 February 2019).

48 *ICE Thinks: Inclusive Cities Discussion Paper,* pp 2, 12.

49 CIC, *Essential Principles for Built Environment Professionals: Creating an Accessible and Inclusive Environment*, Construction Industry Council, London, 2017, http://cic.org.uk/projects/project.php?s=essential-principles-guide (accessed 11 February 2019), p 2.

Conclusion

1 United Nations Convention on the Rights of Persons with Disabilities, Committee on the Rights of Persons with Disabilities, General comment No. 6 (2018) on equality and non-discrimination, https://tbinternet.ohchr.org/_layouts/treatybodyexternal/Download.aspx?symbolno=CRPD/C/GC/6&Lang=en (accessed 14 February 2019)

Further information

1 https://www.gov.uk/government/publications/built-environment-
   professional-education-project-progress-report (accessed 11 February
   2019).
2 http://cic.org.uk/projects/project.php?s=essential-principles-guide
   (accessed 11 February 2019).
3 https://www.london.gov.uk/what-we-do/planning/implementing-london-
   plan/planning-guidance-and-practice-notes/creating-london (accessed 11
   February 2019); see also https://www.islington.gov.uk/planning/planning-
   policy/supplementary-planning-documents/inclusivedesign (accessed 11
   February 2019); see also https://secure.manchester.gov.uk/downloads/
   download/5366/design_for_access_2 (accessed 11 February 2019).
4 https://www.accessassociation.co.uk (accessed 11 February 2019).
5 http://www.nrac.org.uk (accessed 11 February 2019).
6 https://www.designcouncil.org.uk/what-we-do/built-environment/inclusive-
   environments (accessed 11 February 2019).
7 https://cae.org.uk (accessed 11 February 2019).
8 https://www.disabilityrightsuk.org (accessed 11 February 2019).
9 https://www.habinteg.org.uk/fah18 (accessed 11 February 2019).
10 https://www.leonardcheshire.org/about-us/latest-news/press-releases/
   hidden-housing-crisis-severely-limiting-disabled-peoples (accessed 11
   February 2019); see also https://www.leonardcheshire.org/about-us/
   latest-news/press-releases/more-8-10-disabled-people-face-difficulties-
   pubs-and-bars#_#source) (accessed 11 February 2019).

Index

Page numbers in **bold** indicate figures.

5 Pancras Square, King's Cross, London 187–8, **188**

A

Access Adaptations Programme (AAP), City of London 64–7, 75, 77, 80, 81
Access Association 32
Access Committee for England (ACE) 29, 32, 54, 113, 235
anti-discrimination legislation 22, 53–6, **58–9**, 166, 213–14, 226, 243–5
attitude and behaviour change 248–85
   collective and co-production 257–8
   costs of not being inclusive 269–80
   disability employment gap 278–9
   improving skills and knowledge 258–69
   inclusion champions 279–80
   local and strategic access groups 255–6
   lottery funding 276–8

B

Bank of England Museum, City of London 177–9, **178**
Beach Huts, Boscombe, Bournemouth 193–5, **194**, **195**
Birmingham Library 189, **189**
blind and partially sighted people 47, 49, 79–80, 109, 240, 270
BRE Environmental Assessment Method (BREEAM) 228–30
British Standard Codes of Practice 23, 25, 33, 52–3, 113, 116, 201, 219, 221, 234, 235
building regulations 26, 29–30, 46–8, 49, 52, **58–9**, 200–1, 217–20, 235
   Part M 26, 47, 52, 83, 86, 213–14, 217–19, 235, 236
Built Environment Access Panel (BEAP) 100–2, 103–4, 105, 107, 255
Built Environment Professional Education Project (BEPE) 259–64

C

Centre for Accessible Environments (CAE) 32, 50, 55–6, 113
Changing Places toilets 26–7, **27**, 217
Chartered Institution of Highways and Transportation (CIHT) 79, 241–2, 262

Chester 232, **233**
   Storyhouse 146–55, **148**, **149**, **150**, **151**, **152**, **154**
Chobham Manor, Queen Elizabeth Olympic Park, London 113, **114**, **115**, **116**
Chronically Sick and Disabled Persons Act (CSDP Act, 1970) 28–9, 30, 33
City of London Access Group 77–81, 87
City of London Corporation 62, 64–91, 166, 181–2, 192, 225–6
civil rights legislation *see* anti-discrimination legislation
Clink Street, Bankside, London 190–1, **191**
Commission for Architecture and the Built Environment (CABE) 38, 50, 193
Connaught Water, Epping Forest 75, **75**
Construction Industry Council (CIC) 187, 221, 263–4, 266, 279–80, 283
co-production 257–8

D

Dairy, Cottage in the Dales, Yorkshire 272–4, **275**
Deaf people and people with hearing loss 47, 49, 109, 270
   see also Frank Barnes School for Deaf Children, King's Cross, London
DeafSpace Project (DSP) 132–4
DEC! (Design Engineer Construct!) 266–7
Design and Access Statements 38, 104, 117, 166
Design Council 264–5
'design for special needs' approach 25–7, 47–8
Disability Advisory Service 54
Disability Discrimination Act (DDA, 1995) 22, 53–6, 213–14
Disability Rights Commission (DRC) 50, 54–5
Disability Rights Task Force 54
Disabled Persons Act (1981) 33, 217
Disabled Persons Transport Advisory Committee (DPTAC) 50, 113
dropped kerbs 63, 64, 77, 78–81, 88, 110

E

entrances and doors 86–7, **86**, 207–8, **208**
Epping Forest 75–6, **75**, **76**, **77**
Equality Act (2010) 22, 56, 166, 213–14, 226, 243–5
Equality and Human Rights Commission (EHRC) 55, 235–6

F

Frank Barnes School for Deaf Children, King's Cross, London 132–5, **136**, **137**, **138**, **139**

G

Global Disability Innovation Hub (GDIH) 107, 267
Greater London Authority (GLA) 40–6, 98, 106, 111–12, 113
green spaces 75–6
Guildhall, City of London **65**, 67–71, **68**, **69**, **70**, **71**, **72**, **73**, **74**

H

Hammersmith and Fulham Council 257–8
handrails, foreshortened 198–9, **199**
HOME, Manchester 156–61, **156**, **157**, **158**, **159**, **160**
hotels and travel industry 108, 109, 112, 271–4
housing access 28–30, 49, 216, 217–19, 234–7

I

ICE (Institution of Civil Engineers) 259, 262–3, 276, 283
inclusion champions 279–80
inclusive design principles 49–53
inclusive design strategies 220–4

K

kerbs, dropped 63, 64, 77, 78–81, 88, 110
King's Cross Academy, London 132–5, **136**

L

legislation, regulations and technical standards 22–57, **58–9**, 212–45
    access to housing 28–30, 49, 216, 217–19, 234–7
    anti-discrimination legislation 22, 53–6, **58–9**, 166, 213–14, 226, 243–5
    British Standard Codes of Practice 23, 25, 33, 52–3, 113, 116, 201, 219, 221, 234, 235
    building regulations 26, 29–30, 46–8, 49, 52, **58–9**, 200–1, 217–20, 235

'design for special needs' approach 25–7, 47–8

existing and listed buildings 231–2, **233**

inclusive design principles 49–53

inclusive design strategies 220–4

licensing legislation 224–7

local authority access officers 32, 33, 34, 39–40

planning policies 29–30, 33–40, 214–16, 217

social model of disability 30–1, 252

street design 238–43

sustainable design 227–30

see also London Plan

licensing legislation 224–7

Lifetime Homes 29, 30, 234–5

Liverpool Philharmonic Hall 140–4, **142**, **144**, **145**, **146**

local access groups 32, 255–6

Built Environment Access Panel (BEAP) 100–2, 103–4, 105, 107, 255

City of London Access Group 77–81, 87

Corporate Disability Access Forum (CDAF), Cheshire 256

Stratford City Consultative Access Group (SCCAG) 99–101, 104

local authority access officers 32, 33, 34, 39–40

London 62–91

5 Pancras Square, King's Cross 187–8, **188**

Bank of England Museum 177–9, **178**

Chobham Manor, Queen Elizabeth Olympic Park 113, **114**, **115**, **116**

Clink Street, Bankside 190–1, **191**

Epping Forest 75–6, **75**, **76**, **77**

Frank Barnes School for Deaf Children, King's Cross 132–5, **136**, **137**, **138**, **139**

Guildhall **65**, 67–71, **68**, **69**, **70**, **71**, **72**, **73**, **74**

National Army Museum, Chelsea 169–74, **169**, **170**, **171**, **172**, **173**, **174**

O2 Arena, Greenwich 184–6, **186**

St Bartholomew's Hospital 78–9

St Botolph Without Aldgate 83–4, **83**, **84**

St Paul's Cathedral 80, 161–8, **162**, **163**, **165**, **167**

Temple of Mithras 175–6, **176**

Thames Riverside Walk at Blackfriars Bridge 179–83, **180**, **181**, **182**, **183**

Thames Tideway Tunnel 181, 182–3, **183**

Tower Bridge 192–3, **192**

Wood Street Police Station **66**, 67

Woolgate Exchange Building, Basinghall Street **204**, 205

London 2012 Olympic and Paralympic Games 94–117, 165, 252

  compliance procedure 104–5

  direct involvement of disabled people 99–101, 105–7

  going beyond regulations 94–8

  inclusive development process 112–17

  inclusive planning process 98–104

  volunteers 111

  welcoming disabled visitors to London 108–12, 190

London Legacy Development Corporation (LLDC) 101, 104, 105, 107, 113, 255

London Organising Committee of the Olympic and Paralympic Games (LOCOG) 95–6, 97, 106–7, 111, 112

London Plan 40–6, 98, 99, 104, 112, 113, 239, 240

lottery funding 276–8

N

National Army Museum, Chelsea, London 169–74, **169**, **170**, **171**, **172**, **173**, **174**

National Planning Policy Framework (NPPF) 215–16

National Register of Access Consultants (NRAC) 56, 113

O

O2 Arena, Greenwich, London 184–6, **186**

Olympic and Paralympic Games 190, 252–3

  see also London 2012 Olympic and Paralympic Games

Olympic Delivery Authority (ODA) 95, 96, 97, 98, 100, 102–7, 112, 255

P

paving, tactile 63, 64–7, 78–81, **204**
Planning and Compulsory Purchase Act (2004) 38
planning policies 29–30, 33–40, 214–16, 217
   see also building regulations; London Plan
Portway Lifestyle Centre, Sandwell, West Midlands 128–9, **130**, **131**
public transport 85
   ICE 88–9
pubs and restaurants 226–7, 243–4

Q

Queen Elizabeth Olympic Park, London **96**, 101, 116–17
Queen Elizabeth's Hunting Lodge, Epping Forest 75–6, **76**, **77**

R

regulations *see* legislation, regulations and technical standards
restaurants and pubs 226–7, 243–4
RIBA (Royal Institute of British Architects) 261
RIBA Plan of Works 113
Royal Liverpool Philharmonic 140–4, **142**, **144**, **145**, **146**
Royal Society of Arts 265
Royal Town Planning Institute (RTPI) 35

S

seating and benches 205–6, **205**, **206**
'shared space' schemes 239, 240–3, 262
Sill National Landscape Discovery Centre, Northumberland 121–6, **121**, **122**, **126**, **127**, **128**
social model of disability 30–1, 252
St Bartholomew's Hospital, City of London 78–9
St Botolph Without Aldgate, City of London 83–4, **83**, **84**
St Paul's Cathedral, City of London 80, 161–8, **162**, **163**, **165**, **167**
standards *see* legislation, regulations and technical standards
steps and staircases

    foreshortened handrails 198–9, **199**
    highlighting step nosing 200–2, **201**, **202**
    open risers 200, **200**
    surface of 202–3
    tapering 196–7, **197**, **198**
Storyhouse, Chester 146–55, **148**, **149**, **150**, **151**, **152**, **154**
Stratford City Consultative Access Group (SCCAG) 99–101, 104
street design 90–1
    dropped kerbs 63, 64, 77, 78–81, 88, 110
    obstacles and hazards 88, 203–5, **203**, **204**
    seating and benches 205–6, **205**, **206**
    'shared space' schemes 239, 240–3, 262
    tactile paving 63, 64–7, 78–81, **204**
    wayfinding 110, 206–7
    see also steps and staircases
surfaces
    highly patterned and shiny 209
    of steps and staircases 202–3
    tactile paving 63, 64–7, 78–81, **204**
sustainable design 227–30

T

technical standards *see* legislation, regulations and technical standards
Temple of Mithras, City of London 175–6, **176**
Thames Riverside Walk at Blackfriars Bridge, City of London 179–83, **180**, **181**, **182**, **183**
Thames Tideway Tunnel, City of London 181, 182–3, **183**
toilet facilities 25–7, **27**, 63–4, **78**, 79, 217, 239–40
Tower Bridge, London 192–3, **192**

U

United Nations 227–8, 230
Universal Design 49–50

V

View Visitor Centre, Epping Forest 76, **77**

W

Wandsworth Borough Council 34, 77
Wandsworth Disablement Association (WDA) 34, 77
wayfinding 110, 206–7
wedding ceremonies 225–6
Wood Street Police Station, City of London **66**, 67
Woolgate Exchange Building, Basinghall Street, London **204**, 205

Image credits

ABIR Architects / Richard Rowland	Figures 4.72, 4.73
BDP Architects	Figures 4.53–55
BDP / Nick Caville	Figure 4.51
BDP / Paul Rafferty	Figures 4.48–49, 4.52
Bennetts Associates	Figures 4.34–35
Bennetts Associates / Hufton & Crow	Figure 4.67
Bennetts Associates / Mark Carline	Figures 4.28–29, 4.33
Bennetts Associates / Peter Cook	Figures 4.27, 4.30–32
Bennetts Associates / Whybrow	Figure 4.68
Caroe Architecture Ltd	Figures 4.46-47
Caruso St John Architects	Figures 4.22-25
Caruso St John Architects / David Bonnett Associates	Figure 4.26
Cheshire West and Chester Council	Figures 5.2, 6.1
Chris Harrowell	Figure 4.16, 4.19
Chris Wright Photography Ltd / Cottage in the Dales Ltd.	Figures 6.4–5
Crown copyright; published by Office for Disability Issues.	Figure 6.2
David Bonnett Associates	Figures 3.4
David Bonnett Associates / Tamara Kocan	Figure 3.3
David Dropkin	Figure 4.66
David Morris	Figure 1.1
Gethyn Davies	Figure 5.1
Greater London Authority	Figure 1.3
James Newton	Figure 4.56
JDDK Architects	Figures 4.5–8
Julie Fleck	Figures 2.1–3, 2.6, 2.12–20, 3.1, 3.5–7, 4.13–15, 4.17, 4.42–23, 4.45, 4.50, 4.57–58, 4.69–71, 4.74–77, 4.79–84, 4.86, 5.3, 6.6

Kurt Gagen	Figures 4.62–63
LLDC / Rahil Ahmed	Figure 4.85
Margaret Hickish	Figure 3.2
Martin McConaghy IDACS (UK) Ltd	Figure 4.78
Mecanoo Architects	Figures 4.36-41
Neil Smith and Julie Fleck	Figure 1.4
PRP Architects	Figures 3.8, 3.11
PRP Architects / Clive Smith	Figure 3.9
PRP Architects / Richard Chivers	Figure 3.10
Purcell Architects	Figures 2.4–5, 2.7–11
Ron McCrossen	Figures 4.20–21
Sally Ann Norman Photography	Figures 4.1–4
Sam Boone and John Haylett, Clacton School / Class of Your Own	Figure 6.3
St Paul's Cathedral	Figure 4.44
The Design Buro	Figures 4.9–12
Tideway	Figures 4.59–61, 4.64–65

Publishers Note

This main text of this book has been designed and typeset using the sans-serif font Arial, in 13 point. The book has also been printed on uncoated paper to help improve legibility.

Published by RIBA Publishing, 66 Portland Place, London, W1B 1NT

ISBN 978-1-85946-852-4/
EPUB 978-1-85946-912-5

The rights of Julie Fleck as the author of this Work has been asserted in accordance with the Copyright, Designs and Patents Act 1988 sections 77 and 78.

British Library Cataloguing-in-Publication Data
A catalogue record for this book is available from the British Library.

Commissioning Editor: Ginny Mills

Assistant Editor: Clare Holloway

Production: Jane Rogers

Designed and Typeset by Mercer Design, London

Printed and bound by Short Run Press Limited, Exeter

Cover image: Kasia Serafin – AgencyRush.com

While every effort has been made to check the accuracy and quality of the information given in this publication, neither the Author nor the Publisher accept any responsibility for the subsequent use of this information, for any errors or omissions that it may contain, or for any misunderstandings arising from it.

www.ribapublishing.com